RISOTTO

Risotti

Also by Judith Barrett:

Risotto (coauthor)
Cooking Vegetables the Italian Way
Pasta Verde

RISOTTO

Judith Barrett

Macmillan • USA

For David

MACMILLAN
A Simon & Schuster Macmillan Company
1633 Broadway
New York, NY 10019

MACMILLAN is a registered trademark of Macmillan, Inc.

Library of Congress Cataloging-in-Publication Data
   Barrett, Judith, 1948–
     Risotto risotti / by Judith Barrett.
         p.   cm.
    ISBN 0-02-860357-5
    1. Cookery (Rice)   2. Risotto.   3. Cookery,
Italian—Northern style.   I. Title.
TX809.R5B366—1996
641.6'318—dc20   95-50558
                                 CIP

Manufactured in the United States of America
10 9 8 7 6 5 4 3 2 1

BOOK DESIGN AND ILLUSTRATIONS BY MICHELE LASEAU

ACKNOWLEDGMENTS

I am grateful to the many people who helped and encouraged me in the researching and writing of *Risotto Risotti*: Sam Spektor and Ann Berman; Judy and Marvin Zeidler; Didi Emmons; Cliff Wright; Magda and Sergio Brosio; Mary Taylor Simeti; Paul Farber; Renato Campanini; Romano Tamani; Rino and Lucia Botte; Nadia and Antonio Santini; Michael Chiarello and Kevin Cronin; Michel Richard; Maureen and Mauro Vincente; Terrence Brennan; and my good friends who tasted and tested the recipes. I am especially indebted to Pam Hoenig; Jane Sigal; Doe Coover; and my family, David, Annie, and Rachel.

CONTENTS

INTRODUCTION

In the years since *Risotto* (the book) was first published, risotto (the dish) has gone from a barely known ethnic specialty to a popular, almost-mainstream food that can now be found in countless restaurants, Italian or not, from simple diners to elegant establishments, and even on the 24-hour menu of at least one Los Angeles hotel I know.

Risotto helped to make that transition, but so did restaurateurs and chefs who embraced this versatile dish, changed it to meet the demands of restaurant cooking, began serving it in new and different ways, and embellished it with a wild variety of flavorings and ingredients from far beyond Italian culinary boundaries. This in turn educated and excited diners.

Risotto Risotti picks up where *Risotto* left off, adding to the repertoire of classic risotto recipes and at the same time presenting new ways of preparing and serving risotto.

What I discovered in the process of writing this book is that what seems new is sometimes in fact quite old or at least rooted in tradition. And what appears to be typically American is an idea also embraced by Italian cooks. Of the 100 recipes in this book, the vast majority have been inspired by traditional Italian—if not classic risotto—cooking, even some that don't seem Italian at all. For example, "risotto cakes" (cooked, pan-fried risotto patties), one of the most popular American forms of risotto, are actually an adaptation of the traditional Italian risotto pancake, *risotto al salto*. Here they have become a favorite as an accompaniment to main course dishes; in Italy they are served unadorned as a first course with a hefty sprinkling of parmesan cheese.

The recipes for riceless "risotto," which are made using grains other than rice or small diced vegetables without any grains at all, aren't totally new since farro (a type of whole wheat) and barley risotto have been prepared in Italy for a very long time. Low-fat risotto is an idea I thought was purely American, but I found plenty of Italians who cook risotto with little or no added fat.

Some of the so-called new techniques are borrowed from Italy, too. Short-cut risotto is not what most Lombardian chefs are cooking, but at least one, Lucia Botte, at the restaurant Cerasole in Cremona, prepares a no-stir risotto that cooks in 15 minutes and is as creamy and as al dente as any risotto I have ever tasted. And oven-baked risotto, a quicker method that frees the cook from standing and stirring the pot, is an idea I discovered in a Milanese trattoria, where it is called *risotto al forno*.

In all fairness, I have created some unconventional recipes inspired by cuisines where rice is a staple: Asian, North and South American, Middle Eastern, Indian, and Eastern European. Please don't be shocked. You can replace traditional chopped onion with ginger, scallion, and garlic for the beginnings of a Chinese-flavored risotto. When you add a ginger- and soy-seasoned broth, it completes the transition. Similarly, some chopped chilies and fresh cilantro can give risotto a South American taste. For an Asian twist, risotto can be prepared with a lemongrass broth, some coconut milk, and fish sauce. Because risotto is so versatile and lends itself perfectly to so many flavors, I have included a variety of recipes throughout the book to demonstrate just how global risotto can be.

Ultimately, I decided that if you can do it well, then it's worth doing. What's important to me is how good the risotto tastes.

Buon risotto!

risotto
Reference
Guide

What Is Risotto?

At its most basic, risotto is an Italian rice dish made with particular strains of short-grain rice, broth, and other ingredients that give it flavor. But with its incomparable consistency of firm rice grains bound in a velvety sauce, risotto is hardly ordinary.

What gives risotto its singular quality are the particular variety of rice and other ingredients and the specific technique by which they are combined. The starch in the highly glutinous short-grain rice thickens the broth, which is added in small increments, and creates a natural sauce that should be creamy and smooth, never stiff or pasty. In Italy they call the texture of a perfectly cooked risotto, *all'onda*, which means "with waves."

At the same time, the rice is not cooked until soft; rather it is prepared al dente; the grains and should be firm, but not crunchy at the core, or "soul" as the Italians call it, when it is served immediately after it is cooked. It is the unique texture and consistency that make risotto unlike any other rice dish in the world.

History

Rice, one of the first grains ever to be cultivated, has been the most important food staple for over half the world's population for thousands of years. Where and when rice first came to the Italian peninsula is not definite. One theory is that the ancient Greeks brought rice to the Italian peninsula when they settled in Southern Italy. There is evidence of the use of rice in ancient Rome in the writings of Horace, Pliny, and Columella who all celebrated the health benefits of a drink made from rice.

After the eighth century A.D. and the Saracen invasion of the Italian peninsula, rice became an established Italian foodstuff. It was not cultivated on a large scale, however, until at least the end of the thirteenth century when the dukes of Milan took an interest in rice and brought it to the Po River delta in Lombardy. It is there that the rice growing and processing industry grew up and still thrives. Today Italy is the largest producer of rice in western Europe, growing not only the short-grain varieties for risotto but long-grain varieties for export as well.

Because of risotto's affinity with Near Eastern pilaf (both dishes call for the rice to be cooked with onion or other flavorings and broth), some historians say that risotto originated near Venice, a city known for its contacts with the Levant. Others contend it was a southern Italian invention.

Perhaps the best-known legend of the first risotto harks back to 1574. The story goes that during the 200 years of the construction of the *duomo*, Milan's fabulous marble-spired cathedral, temporary housing for the workers, who came from all parts of Europe, was erected behind the church. Among the community of Belgians was Valerius, a master glass worker who was in charge of executing the stained glass for the cathedral. One of his apprentices had gained a reputation for his color-mixing virtuosity, and rumor had it that he had achieved his lustrous colors by adding a pinch of saffron to his pigments. When he added saffron to the rice at Valerius' daughter's wedding, the guests are said to have exclaimed, "*Risus optimus*," which in Latin means, "excellent rice." The yellow rice soon became known as *risotto alla milanese*, which is still made with a hefty pinch of saffron.

To this day, risotto remains a specialty of the northern Italian regions of Piedmont, Lombardy, the Veneto, Trentino-Alto Adige, and Friuli, where it figures prominently in everyday eating as well as on restaurant menus. But risotto is also prepared in Italy well beyond the borders of these regions. You can find risotto in almost every part of Italy, even as far south as Sicily, although the preparations inevitably reflect the local ingredients, and traditional cooking styles differ in flavoring and texture from region to region.

Ingredients

Rice

Rice, a semiaquatic member of the grass family, is the basic ingredient of risotto, as the name suggests. "*Riso*" means rice in Italian. (Risotto is the dish and "risotti" is the plural of risotto.) But not all types of rice are suited to the preparation of risotto. The type of rice that is best for risotto is short-grain rice because it has the highest proportion of amylopectin, the glutinous starch found in rice that produces the creamy texture associated with a traditional risotto. And only certain strains of short-grain rice are considered good for preparing risotto. The Italian-grown Arborio, Vialone, Carnaroli, and Baldo are the principal rices used for preparing risotto and can be used interchangeably, though with experience of the various rice strains, you will be able to discern subtle differences in grain size, cooking time, and texture.

Rice for risotto is grown throughout Lombardy and Piedmont and processed locally there in *riserie*, rice factories. Some are large and run by big corporations, others are small family-run establishments. On a visit to Mantova (a town in Lombardy) while working on this book, I visited the Riseria Campanini, a small 60-year-old company still run by the founder and his two sons. Campanini produces only Vialone and Carnaroli rice, which are typical of Mantovana cooking (western Lombardy and Piedmont are known for growing Arborio rice).

The Campanini rice fields are flooded in the spring for planting and growing and then drained and dried in the fall before the harvest. The harvested rice is brought to the factory to be hulled, cleaned, sorted, polished, and packaged. Rice processing at Campanini is done with heavy machinery, but the Campanini brothers and workers still must exercise their visual judgment and expertise in producing the finished product because there is an important but fine line in the processing of rice for risotto: The grains of rice must be white but not so polished they lose their starchy coating, which is essential to a perfect risotto.

The short-grain rice called for in most of the recipes in this book is Arborio because it is the most widely available and the most economical of the Italian risotto rices sold in the United States. Originally produced from a cross between Vialone and an American strain called Lady Wright, Arborio's grains are generally wider and longer than the other short-grain rices. Arborio is also considered the least forgiving of the risotto rices because it has only a momentary time span during which it will be perfectly cooked, tender on the outside and firm on the inside, before it becomes soft and overcooked.

Carnaroli and Vialone are also excellent choices for preparing risotto, but since they are grown in smaller quantities and not exported as widely as Arborio, they are more expensive and less easy to find. Carnaroli, like Arborio, is a hybrid of two rice strains, Vialone and Lencino. It has the most tapered grain of the three risotto rices. It tends to cook uniformly and is more resistant to overcooking than Arborio and therefore is also used in other nonrisotto rice dishes. Vialone, grown only in a narrow region between Lombardy and the Veneto, is the oldest of the

rice varieties and has the roundest, shortest grain. It can absorb twice its own grain weight in liquid and for this reason it is considered by many Italian cooks to be the best, ideal rice for risotto.

Baldo, a rice variety that is becoming more popular and available in the United States, is grown in Piedmont and is considered to be comparable to Arborio both in shape and cooking quality. There are several other less-known Italian rice varieties but they are not generally available in the United States.

The only acceptable substitutes for Italian-grown rice are American short-grain, California-grown Arborio and "pearl" rice. Short-grain California Arborio rice is available in health-food markets. "Pearl" rice is sold in Asian markets as sushi, Chinese, or Nishiki rice, and in Spanish/Latin supermarkets as Valencia rice. It is glutinous enough to produce an approximation of the consistency of a traditional risotto: The grains remain firm and the broth thickens. However, the finished texture of the risotto made with these rices is less creamy than a traditional risotto. In some of the recipes that follow, particularly the recipes with Asian, Latin American, or Spanish flavorings, American short-grain rice is specifically called for, and it can always be used as a substitute for Arborio rice if Italian rice is not available.

None of the long-grain rices, white or brown, including Basmati and Texmati rice, are suitable for preparing risotto. Where the short-grain rice has a high proportion of amylopectin, or glutinous starch, the long-grain rice has a high ratio of amylose, the type of starch that makes long-grain rice cook up with the grains separate and fluffy. These rice varieties cook very quickly, making the grains excessively soft for risotto. And they are not sufficiently glutinous to yield the proper creamy consistency. They can give you a tasty rice dish, but it won't be risotto.

Finally, although the word risotto implies that rice is in the recipe, today it is not unheard of for a dish called "risotto" to be prepared without rice, using other grains such as pearl barley, whole wheat in the form of farro, or pasta, or without any grain whatsoever, using vegetables, particularly potatoes, that have been diced into small, almost grain-size pieces. For these dishes, the name "risotto" is always in quotes and refers to the preparation technique—they are prepared in the manner of a risotto. (See Chapter Nine, "Riceless 'Risotti,'" pages 177–89.)

Rice and most other grains should be kept in an airtight container, preferably in the refrigerator, and should be used within six months to a year. Rice that's been sitting around for many months may not produce the same creamy texture that more recently harvested rice produces. Since there is no way to tell how old or newly packaged the rice is that you buy, it's best to buy rice only when you intend to use it and not keep it around for long periods.

Olive Oil

More than half the recipes in this book are rooted in Italian cooking and call for olive oil. While you can substitute other oils, olive oil gives these dishes the distinctive flavor associated with traditional risotto.

Throughout the centuries, olive oil has maintained a prominent place in Italian culture, as well as its cuisine. We know that the Romans used olive oil for many nonculinary purposes, but it is in Italian cooking that olive oil has achieved and maintained, over thousands of years, its most important status.

The process by which olive oil is made today is essentially the same as it has been for centuries: The olives, pits and all, are crushed and ground to a paste. Next, the olive paste is spread onto filters, which are stacked into a press, and the oil is pressed out. While all olive oil is pressed in generally this same manner, many factors determine the quality and flavor of the finished product.

Like wine in Italy, olive oil and its production are government regulated and the different oils are classified. The best olive oil, labeled *extra-virgin*, has an acidity level of less than 1 percent and is generally made from the first pressing of the highest quality olives (overripe or bruised olives raise the acidity level and lower the quality of the oil). Within the category of extra-virgin oils, however, there are still more distinctions and quality standards based on such factors as whether the oil is filtered or unfiltered, cold or hot pressed, or whether any chemicals or additives are used. In addition, the size, age, location, and modernity of the *frantoio* or factory where the oil is pressed and the *oleoficio* where the oil is packed into bottles also affect the quality of the oil. (Since olive oils from countries other than Italy are not subjected to these regulations, labels such as "extra-virgin" may not have the same meaning as it does for Italian oils.)

Most of what is exported to the United States is called *pure* olive oil; it is refined olive oil with a higher acidity level. Made from the second and third pressings of olives, from the first pressing of lesser-quality olives, or even from the pressing of the olive pits, pure olive oil starts out with an acidity level between 3 and 4 percent. Called *lampante*, it is refined in factories to remove impurities and ultimately lower the acidity level to below 3 percent. Before bottling, a small percentage of extra-virgin oil is added to the refined oil to give it color and flavor. The differences among pure olive oils come primarily from the quantity and quality of extra-virgin oil that is added to it.

I like to use a moderately priced Italian extra-virgin olive oil in cooking because it is unadulterated and has a distinctive but not overpowering flavor. I reserve the more expensive oils for salads or drizzling on bread or soups.

Olive oil will keep for many months in a cool, dark place. An unopened container can keep for as long as two years. If you buy the oil by the gallon, you should transfer a small quantity—about a quart of oil—to a serving container for daily use.

Canola Oil

Also called rapeseed oil, canola oil is mono-unsaturated and has the distinction of being the oil that contains the lowest saturated fat and the highest unsaturated fat of any edible oil. Flavorless, colorless, and odorless, it has a high smoking point and is well suited to cooking, although it won't add any flavor to your risotto. For anyone concerned, for health reasons, with the type of oil used in risotto, canola is an acceptable substitute to olive oil.

Butter

In Italy unsalted butter is used liberally in the preparation of risotto and greatly enhances both the flavor and creamy consistency of the finished dish. Especially in seafood risotti where cheese is not added to the rice, the addition of butter just before serving is essential to achieving the right texture.

Just how much butter is typically added at the end? As one Italian chef told me, a "walnut-sized" piece per serving is stirred into risotto at the end of the cooking. I calculate that to be about 2 tablespoons per serving.

In the interest of health, I have tried to keep the quantity of butter to a minimum. You can also eliminate the butter completely. (See Chapter Seven, "Low-Fat Risotti," pages 133–50.)

Parmesan Cheese

A majority of the recipes in this book call for "Italian parmesan" cheese to be stirred into the risotto, or sprinkled on top when the risotto is served at the table. "Parmesan" is the American name for the Italian parmigiano, which more accurately is parmigiano-reggiano, a particular cheese made in a specific area of Italy under certain conditions and with explicitly defined ingredients, all regulated by the Italian government. However, it has come to refer to a host of cheeses that are like parmigiano-reggiano.

Unless specified otherwise, I recommend using the authentic parmigiano-reggiano cheese wherever "Italian parmesan" is called for, because I think it melts better, giving the finished risotto the desired texture. And even more important, with its nutty, mild, and only slightly salty flavor, it tastes better.

Parmigiano-reggiano is a handmade product that has been produced continuously in the same manner for over 700 years in *caseifici*, small cheese factories, and only in a narrowly defined area around Parma, Reggio-Emilia, Modena, Bologna, and Mantova.

The milk, gathered from two milkings a day, is partially skimmed and augmented with whey from the previous day's cheese-making to encourage fermentation. The cheese is curdled with rennet. The curds are drained and weighted in large round molds, which give the cheese its shape. When firm enough, the cheeses are removed from the molds, air dried, causing the rind to form, then soaked in heavily salted water, which both preserves and flavors the cheese. The end products are 60- to 70-pound wheels of cheese—each bearing its production date and the parmigiano-reggiano logo imprinted on it. The cheeses are then aged for eighteen months to two years. The longer the cheese ages, the drier it is.

If parmigiano-reggiano is not available, use a substitute. The best substitute is the Italian grana cheese, which is very much like the parmigiano-reggiano but is manufactured outside the government-designated area. It is made mostly in large factories (not by hand) in Lombardy and Piedmont, and it is produced in much bigger quantities with different controls and restrictions. It is, therefore, generally less expensive than its formidable counterpart. Its flavor, while still relatively mild and nutty-tasting, is slightly sharper than parmigiano-reggiano and more salty. Its texture, however, is very similar, and the two cheeses can be used interchangeably in most recipes calling for "Italian parmesan."

There are several types of grana, but in the United States it is grana padano (padano meaning *from the Po River*) from Piedmont and Lombardy that is most available. Grana lodigiano is from the town of Lodi in southern Lombardy, and grana piacentino comes from the town of Piacenza, also in Lombardy.

Parmesan-type cheeses from countries other than Italy, including Argentina and the United States, produce inferior products, and

I would only recommend these if there are no Italian varieties available.

If you buy parmesan already grated, it may lose freshness within a week in your refrigerator. It's best to buy parmesan by the piece and grate it just before you intend to use it. If you do buy grated cheese, you can store it in the freezer and defrost it before using. Freeze in small containers.

Salt

I prefer to use—and recommend—kosher salt in cooking. It is unadulterated; no iodine is added as it is in table salt. I like the relatively large crystals of kosher salt making it easy to sprinkle with your fingers, which I find to be a more controlled and therefore preferable method of salting compared to pouring or sprinkling from a salt shaker. I also like the saltiness of kosher salt—it's not too salty the way sea salt is and yet it's plenty salty enough.

I do not specify kosher salt in the recipes that follow. I strongly recommend using it, but you can use whatever salt you have on hand.

Essential Equipment

The Risotto Pot

The most essential piece of equipment for making risotto is a good pot. What constitutes a good pot? It should be large enough to hold the finished risotto, which means at least

a 4-quart size, and it must be constructed of heavy, flameproof materials that will heat the pot evenly and hold the heat continuously throughout the cooking time without overheating in some spots causing the rice to stick and burn. Ordinary saucepans are typically heavier on the bottom than on the sides and therefore cook unevenly—the sides will be hotter than the bottom. In addition, single-handled saucepans are generally not recommended because most conventional saucepans are typically 2- to 3-quart size, and most of the risotto recipes that follow call for a larger pot, 4-quart size or bigger.

My favorite pots for risotto include heavy, enameled cast-iron oven casseroles (such as Le Creuset). These work extremely well for preparing risotto, and the enameled interior creates an almost-nonstick surface, making clean-up easier. Also excellent for risotto are heavy copper pots, particularly those with stainless-steel linings, and heavy-gauge all-stainless-steel pots. Nonstick coated aluminum pots can be used provided they are constructed with sufficiently heavy materials.

A Wooden Spoon

In the early days when most cooking was done in copper pans lined with silver or tin, a wooden spoon was essential to protect the pots from becoming scratched. For risotto, a wooden spoon was doubly necessary because it wouldn't break or harm the individual grains of rice. It is for this second reason that wooden spoons with long handles are still called for in the preparation of risotto. In addition, wooden spoons won't become hot or melt from the heat of the stove. A large plastic spoon may be less aesthetically pleasing than wood, but it's OK if it's the cooking kind.

Measuring Cups and Spoons

You will need a selection of measuring cups and spoons. A 2-cup glass measure is the most practical for measuring the rice. You should also have on hand a set of stainless-steel cups that include 1-cup, ½-cup, ⅓-cup and ¼-cup sizes for portioning out the broth and measuring the additional ingredients. A set of measuring spoons will also be useful, although most recipes do not require precise measurement.

Serving Risotto

Traditionally in Italy, risotto, like pasta, is served as a first course before an entrée of fish or meat. But in the United States, risotto is mostly served as the main course. For this reason I have tried to make many of the risotto recipes main-course dishes. Some are in classic form with the meat or fish stirred into the rice, others are served almost as a side dish with meat or fish.

Whether you choose to serve risotto as a first course or entrée, it should be served as soon as it is finished cooking. Leaving it to stand for even 5 minutes will adversely effect the taste and the texture of the risotto: the grains of rice will continue to soak up cooking liquid and become soft; the flowing texture of the risotto will thicken and turn stiff as the grains continue to absorb the liquid; and the risotto will lose heat, and with it some of its delicious flavor.

Whether in soup bowls or on dinner plates, risotto should always be served in preheated dishes so the hot risotto doesn't end up on a cold plate and turn cold before you have a chance to enjoy it. I preheat my stack of serving plates in my microwave for 2 to 3 minutes; you can also put them in a very low, 140 degree oven while you prepare the risotto; they will warm while you cook.

Most recipes in this book are made with 2 cups of raw rice and are meant to serve 4 to 6. That is to say, 4 as a main course and 6 as a first course.

chapter TWO

Risotto Techniques:

the Long and the Short

Classic Risotto

There is an established, specific technique for preparing risotto. This technique will yield a dish of rice with particular characteristics: full-flavored and al dente grains bound in a velvety sauce.

The preparation of classic risotto begins by cooking finely chopped aromatic vegetables such as onion or shallot, celery, carrot, and garlic, or a combination of two or more of these ingredients in butter and/or oil. In Italian this mixture is called a *soffritto*. You want to cook the vegetables to soften but not brown them.

Next, stir the raw, unwashed rice into the *soffritto* and lightly cook it until the grains are well coated with the oil, butter, and onion (or vegetable) mixture and are hot. You don't want to brown the rice, you only want to coat and heat it.

Once the rice is coated and hot, you can begin to add the wine and/or broth. If you are adding wine, it should be at room temperature and added before any broth so that the grains of rice can fully absorb the wine's flavor. The broth must be simmering or very hot. Using hot broth ensures that the risotto cooks at a low, even boil throughout the cooking process. If you add cool or even warm broth, it will lower the temperature of the risotto each time you add some, taking longer for the grains to absorb the liquid and slowing down the overall cooking time if you have to wait for the rice to come back to a boil after each addition of broth. The broth should be added in ½-cup increments.

Most of the time, you cook or partially cook the ingredients that flavor a risotto separately and add them either halfway through or at the end of the cooking process. Some ingredients such as shellfish or some heartier vegetables you add raw to the risotto at various points during the cooking process, depending on the ingredients.

Continue to add the broth in ½-cup increments, stirring almost continuously, until the grains of rice are firm to the bite but tender all the way through, about 20 minutes from the time you add the first addition of liquid (wine or broth).

When the rice is done, turn off the heat. Stir in a final small, about ¼ cup, portion of broth. This addition of broth ensures the finished texture will be velvety and smooth and slightly fluid. Add the flavoring ingredients—cheeses, butter, prepared meat, fish, or vegetables—and vigorously stir to incorporate all the ingredients completely and uniformly into the rice. Taste your risotto and season with salt as necessary.

Serve risotto as soon as it is finished cooking. If left to stand for even a few minutes after cooking, the rice will continue to absorb the liquid and eventually will turn stiff and lose its creamy consistency.

Basic Recipe for Classic Risotto

1. COMBINE 1 tablespoon of the butter and the oil in a heavy 4-quart pot over medium-high heat. Add the onion and cook, stirring with a wooden spoon, until the onion begins to soften, 2 to 3 minutes. Be careful not to brown it. Stir in the rice to coat the grains with the fat and onion mixture, and cook about 1 minute longer.

2. ADD the wine and cook, stirring, until it is mostly absorbed by the rice. Begin to add the broth, ½ cup at a time, stirring well after each addition. Wait until each addition is almost completely absorbed before adding the next ½ cup. Reserve ¼ cup of the broth to add at the end.

3. WHEN the rice is tender but firm, in about 20 minutes, turn off the heat. Add the remaining ¼ cup broth and 1 tablespoon butter, the cheese, salt and pepper to taste, and stir well to combine with the rice. Serve immediately.

2 tablespoons unsalted butter

1 tablespoon olive oil

½ cup finely chopped onion

2 cups Arborio rice

½ cup dry white wine

6 cups chicken broth, preferably homemade (pages 27–28), heated

½ cup freshly grated Italian parmesan cheese

Salt

Freshly ground black pepper

Makes 6 servings

Shortcut Risotti

If there's ever a complaint about risotto, it's that it requires too much stirring, too much attending to, and too much work at the last minute. For cooks who don't want to stand and stir for the full 20 minutes classic risotto requires, there are some alternatives. None of them measures up to the perfectly textured, al dente rice and creamy consistency that is characteristic of classically made risotto, but each will produce a delicious risotto you can be proud to serve.

All of the following shortcut techniques can be applied to the recipes in this book. Wherever there are changes or adjustments to make, they are indicated in the description of the techniques below.

Pressure-Cooker Risotto

Of all the shortcuts and reduced-work techniques for preparing risotto, the pressure-cooker method is my favorite. It's the fastest by far and it produces an almost perfectly textured risotto that's closest to the risotto you get from the classic stand-and-stir technique. Its main drawback, at least for many people, is the pressure cooker itself.

The pressure cooker is, for the multitudes of people who do not use them regularly, a scary object to be avoided. That said, I would encourage you to be brave in the name of simplified risotto. The pressure cookers that are manufactured today are very different from the cookers made in the 1950s and '60s. They are extremely if not completely safe; most come equipped with several safety features which help ensure that you can't make a mistake and hurt yourself. In addition, the better models today are made of heavy stainless steel, which makes them more durable and better to cook with than their predecessors.

Lorna Sass is generally credited with popularizing this pressure-cooker risotto technique in her cookbook, *Cooking Under Pressure* (Morrow) in 1989. But even before, in 1979, Franco and Margaret Romagnoli recommended using the pressure cooker for preparing risotto in their cookbook, *The New Italian Cooking* (Atlantic-Little Brown). And in my own book, *Risotto*, in 1988, the use of the pressure cooker is recommended.

What we all confirm is that this technique has been around for years. And while it may be surprising to some, Europeans in general have long embraced the pressure cooker for its convenience, and Italians in particular have been using the pressure cooker for making risotto and countless other dishes.

Cooking risotto in the pressure cooker is a lot like cooking risotto in a conventional pot. Both techniques begin and end the same way. But pressure-cooker risotto has some essential differences: Most of the broth is added all at once instead of in increments. Pressure-cooker risotto requires less broth than traditional risotto recipes—the ratio is approximately 2 to 1 (twice as much broth as rice), while traditional recipes call for almost 3 to 1, broth to rice. And although the *soffritto* is cooked in the classic manner, the other risotto flavorings—vegetables, fish, meat, cheeses, etc.—are *always* cooked separately and combined with the risotto after the rice is finished cooking, which means that these ingredients are not overcooked.

Always follow the manufacturer's directions for using your pressure cooker and always follow the cooking time for pressure-cooker risotto exactly: One minute of overcooking in the pressure cooker is the equivalent of about 5 minutes in a conventional pot on top of the stove, and overcooking will mean soggy rice.

Basic Recipe for Pressure-Cooker Risotto

2 tablespoons unsalted butter

1 tablespoon olive oil

½ cup finely chopped onion

2 cups Arborio rice

½ cup dry white wine

4 ½ cups broth of your choice,
  preferably homemade
  (pages 27–33), heated

½ cup freshly grated Italian
  parmesan cheese

Salt

Freshly ground black pepper

Makes 6 servings

1. COMBINE 1 tablespoon of the butter and the oil in the pressure cooker, uncovered, over medium-high heat. Add the onion and cook, stirring with a wooden spoon, until the onion begins to soften, 2 to 3 minutes. Be careful not to brown it. Stir in the rice to coat the grains with the fat and onion mixture, and cook about 1 minute longer.

2. ADD the wine and cook, stirring, until it is mostly absorbed by the rice. Add 4 cups of the broth. Cover the pressure cooker according to the manufacturer's instructions, increase the heat to high, bring the pressure up to full, and cook exactly 5 minutes.

3. TURN off the heat. Place the cooker in the sink and run cold water over the top until the pressure drops completely and all the safety latches indicate the pressure is completely down. Remove the lid.

4. RETURN the cooker, uncovered, to the stove over low heat. Add the remaining ½ cup broth, 1 tablespoon butter, and the cheese and stir well to combine with the rice. Season with salt and pepper to taste. Serve immediately.

Microwave Risotto

The technique of cooking risotto in a micro-wave was invented by the food writer and cookbook author Barbara Kafka and intro-duced in her cookbook, *Microwave Gourmet* (Morrow, 1987). It requires more overall cooking time than the traditional stand-and-stir classic risotto recipe, closer to 30 minutes than 20, but you have to stir the risotto only two or three times in the course of cooking. There is also additional "standing" time once the cooking is completed. You can add flavoring ingredients to the rice and cook them at the same time as the rice.

As with all microwave cooking, smaller quantities cook more quickly than larger amounts: One cup of rice plus broth and other flavoring ingredients will cook in close to 30 minutes; 2 cups of rice will require more than 45 minutes of cooking. In the basic microwave recipe that follows, I have kept Kafka's basic measurements. You can increase the rice to 2 cups, but you will also have to expand the cooking time.

The times given in the recipe that follows are calculated for a 750-watt microwave oven fitted with a carousel. Smaller ovens and ovens without a turntable may require more cooking time.

Basic Recipe for Microwave Risotto

2 tablespoons unsalted butter

1 tablespoon olive oil

½ cup finely chopped onion

1 cup Arborio rice

3 ¼ cups broth of your choice,
   preferably homemade
   (pages 27–33), heated

¼ cup freshly grated Italian
   parmesan cheese

Salt

Freshly ground black pepper

Makes 3 to 4 servings

(Adapted from Microwave Gourmet *by Barbara Kafka)*

1. COMBINE 1 tablespoon of the butter and the oil in a 2-quart glass or ceramic soufflé dish. Heat, uncovered, in the microwave on high until the butter melts, about 2 minutes. Add the onion and stir, using a wooden spoon, to combine with the butter and oil. Cook, uncovered, on high until the onion begins to soften, about 2 minutes. Stir in the rice to coat the grains with the fat and onion mixture, and cook on high 1 minute longer.

2. ADD 3 cups of the broth to the dish with the rice and onion mixture. Stir to combine. Cook uncovered on high for 9 minutes. Stir well. Continue cooking on high 9 minutes longer.

3. REMOVE the dish from the oven. Let stand, covered, 5 minutes, stirring frequently. Uncover the dish, add the remaining ¼ cup broth and 1 tablespoon butter, and the cheese, and stir well to combine with the rice. Season with salt and pepper to taste. Serve immediately.

More-Broth-at-Once Risotto

This technique differs from the classic technique on pages 12–13 in that, as the name implies, the broth is added in greater quantities, using 1-cup additions rather than the classic ½-cup increments. While this technique requires about the same amount of overall cooking time, its prime benefit to the cook is that you don't have to stir continuously. Stirring prevents the rice from sticking to the bottom of the pot.

In classic risotto you stir almost constantly because the small additions of broth are not enough to protect the rice from sticking. With more broth at once, it takes longer for the rice to absorb the broth and cook down to the point where it could stick to the pot. So you stir less. The number of additions of broth is cut by about half, so is the amount of stirring. With this technique, you can almost fully achieve the creamy consistency and al dente grains of classic risotto. Still, as with all the techniques, you have to be careful to not add too much broth and/or overcook the rice. Be sure to cook the risotto at a low, even boil.

To use this technique with any risotto recipe in this book, add the broth in 1-cup increments, adding more broth when the rice is almost completely absorbed by the rice, and cooking until the rice is tender but firm, about 20 minutes from the time you make the first addition of broth to the rice. The overall quantity of broth may be ½ to 1 cup less than is called for in the classic technique.

Restaurant Risotto

Although most of you won't have a reason to prepare risotto the way most American restaurants do, this technique can be adapted for home use. This method will produce a deliciously flavored risotto, but as you may have noted when eating risotto in restaurants, it usually lacks the creaminess associated with the classic risotto.

The technique calls for partially cooking the risotto. After the rice has cooked only 10 minutes, the still-crunchy and fairly soupy rice is poured onto baking sheets, spread into an even layer, and allowed to cool completely. (Spreading out the risotto helps it to cool quickly, which stops the rice from continuing to soften.) When an order for risotto comes into the restaurant kitchen, a portion of the cooled, partially cooked rice is added to boiling broth thereby reconstituting the risotto. The portion of risotto cooks only about five minutes longer, until the rice is tender but firm. The flavorings—such as cheeses, seafood, or vegetables—are added at the end.

While this technique is designed for making individual portions of risotto, it can also be used to prepare up to four portions: Simply add all of the partially cooked risotto to the remaining boiling broth and finish cooking the risotto until the grains are tender but firm. Add the cheese, butter, and any other flavoring ingredients.

Basic Recipe for Restaurant Risotto

2 tablespoons unsalted butter

1 tablespoon olive oil

½ cup finely chopped onion

2 cups Arborio rice

½ cup dry white wine

6 cups chicken broth,
    preferably homemade
    (pages 27–28), heated

½ cup freshly grated Italian
    parmesan cheese

Salt

Freshly ground black pepper

Makes 6 servings

1. Combine 1 tablespoon of butter with the oil in a heavy 4-quart pot over medium-high heat. Add the onion and cook, stirring with a wooden spoon until the onion begins to soften, 2 to 3 minutes. Be careful not to brown it. Stir in the rice to coat the grains with the fat and onion mixture, and cook about 1 minute longer.

2. Add the wine and cook, stirring, until it is mostly absorbed by the rice. Add the broth, ½ cup at a time, stirring well after each addition. Wait until each addition is almost completely absorbed before adding the next ½ cup.

3. When approximately half the broth has been added, after 10 minutes of cooking, pour the risotto onto a foil-lined baking sheet and spread into an even layer to cover most of the sheet. Allow to cool, uncovered, to room temperature. Cover with plastic wrap and refrigerate until ready to finish cooking.

4. About 10 minutes before you plan to serve the risotto, reserve ¼ cup of the broth and reheat all the remaining broth to simmering in a clean heavy 4-quart pot. (You can reuse the pot, above, but it should be washed and cleaned before continuing.) Cut or break the chilled risotto into pieces and add to the broth, stirring vigorously, until all the risotto has been added.

5. Continue stirring until the rice is tender but firm, in about 5 minutes. Turn off the heat. Add the reserved ¼ cup broth, the remaining butter, the cheese, and salt and pepper to taste. Stir well to combine with the rice. Serve immediately.

Risotto *Al Forno*

Baked risotto, or risotto *al forno*, is a great dish to make for company since you can prepare most of it in advance and then finish it in the oven just before you plan to serve it—freeing you from standing and stirring the pot steadily while the rice cooks. As with every short-cut risotto technique, baked risotto is not equal to the classic version. What you lose in the baking process is the trademark risotto consistency: Baked risotto comes out slightly drier and somewhat less creamy. But provided you don't overbake the dish, a baked risotto is a rich rice dish with the all of the flavor and much of the texture of a classic risotto.

The cooking method for baked risotto requires you to start the risotto on top of the stove in the traditional way, cooking the onions with butter and/or oil and the rice. After you add the broth, the risotto goes directly into a preheated oven to bake. You do have to watch the clock closely; baked risotto requires just 15 minutes in the oven—and there isn't much leeway in this recipe; if you overbake by even a minute, the al dente texture associated with risotto will be lost. Because timing is important, it's best to use a kitchen timer. When the risotto is taken from the oven, a final addition of broth is stirred in along with whatever flavoring ingredients you are adding.

Basic Recipe for Baked Risotto

2 tablespoons unsalted butter

1 tablespoon olive oil

½ cup finely chopped onion

2 cups Arborio rice

½ cup dry white wine

3 ½ cups chicken broth,
preferably homemade
(pages 27–28), heated

½ cup freshly grated Italian
parmesan cheese

Salt

Freshly ground black pepper

Makes 4 to 6 servings

1. PREHEAT the oven to 425 degrees.

2. COMBINE 1 tablespoon of the butter and the oil in a heavy 4-quart flameproof casserole with a tight-fitting lid over medium-high heat. Add the onion and cook, stirring with a wooden spoon, until the onion begins to soften, 2 to 3 minutes. Be careful not to brown it. Stir in the rice to coat the grains with the fat and onion mixture, and cook about 1 minute longer.

3. ADD the wine and cook, stirring, until it is mostly absorbed by the rice. Add 3 cups of the broth and stir well to combine. Cover the casserole, place in the oven, and bake exactly 15 minutes.

4. REMOVE the casserole from the oven. Add the remaining ½ cup hot broth. Stir in the cheese, any other cheeses, and any remaining ingredients such as parsley or butter. Season to taste with salt and pepper. Serve immediately.

Almost-No-Stir Risotto

This technique was passed on to me by Rino Botte, the owner of the restaurant Cerasole in Cremona, Italy. I had enjoyed two risotti there that were nothing short of spectacular. When I asked about his recipes, Rino explained that his wife, Lucia, the restaurant's chef, came up with this technique because it allows the rice to cook in 15 minutes instead of the usual 20. And it frees up the cook; it doesn't require the constant stirring of traditional risotto.

As Rino explained, after cooking the *soffritto* and stirring in the rice and wine, the broth is added to the rice over low heat in two additions, half when the rice begins to cook, and the remaining broth halfway through the cooking (after 7 minutes).

You don't stir the rice at all while it's cooking, Botte said, because this allows a thin film to form between the rice and the bottom of the pot which acts to seal in the rice. If you do stir, he explained, it will break the film and cause the rice to stick to the pot and dry out.

After 15 minutes, when almost all the broth has cooked into the rice, and the rice is tender but still al dente, then vigorous stirring is required as you add the final additions of broth, butter, parmesan cheese, and whatever other flavorings are called for in the recipe.

Basic Recipe for Almost-No-Stir Risotto

2 tablespoons unsalted butter

1 tablespoon olive oil

½ cup finely chopped onion

2 cups Arborio rice

½ cup dry white wine

4 cups chicken broth, preferably homemade (pages 27–28), heated

⅓ cup freshly grated Italian parmesan cheese

Salt

Freshly ground black pepper

Makes 4 to 6 servings

1. COMBINE 1 tablespoon of the butter with the oil in a heavy 4-quart pot over medium-high heat. Add the onion and cook, stirring, until it begins to soften, 2 to 3 minutes. Stir in the rice to coat the grains with the fat and onion mixture, and cook about 1 minute longer.

2. ADD the wine and cook, stirring, until it is almost completely absorbed by the rice. Add 2 cups of the broth, stir to combine, reduce the heat to low and cook, uncovered, exactly 7 minutes. Add the remaining 2 cups of broth, without stirring, and cook exactly 7 minutes longer.

3. TURN the heat to medium high, add the remaining tablespoon of butter and the cheese, and stir well to combine with the rice. Season with salt and pepper to taste. Serve immediately.

chapter THREE

Broth
Recipes

$\mathscr{B}$roth is the most important ingredient in risotto after rice, adding more to risotto's delicious taste than any other single ingredient. You should always use a well-flavored, well-seasoned broth—whether it is made with vegetables, fish, shellfish, chicken, or meat—and avoid using broth with a strong or salty taste that could overpower the finished risotto.

In fact, using a salty broth is one of the biggest errors in preparing risotto. Broth cooked in risotto tends to become concentrated as it cooks down and has a tendency to concentrate not only the flavors but the saltiness as well.

Ideally the broth you use should be prepared from scratch with fresh ingredients. However, there are inevitably times when instant bouillon or canned, low-sodium broth will have to do. I often use instant bouillon cubes but I always over-dilute them with water to tone down their distinctive and salty taste. Occasionally I augment the broth I do have on hand with commercially prepared broth or bouillon.

In Italy a chicken or chicken and meat broth is used to prepare most risotto recipes, with the exception of some fish and seafood recipes. But even many of those are prepared with chicken broth. I have left the choice to you, except in a few specific recipes where I think the risotto will be compromised if it is prepared with any broth other than what I have specified; and in the vegetable risotti, which all call for vegetable broth.

Following are variations of broth that are called for in this book. You can always substitute with a broth you have on hand, chicken broth, or even water. Whenever specific substitutions are possible they will be listed in the recipe. Whatever broth you do use, be sure to taste it and make sure you like the taste of it because it will be the dominant flavor of your risotto.

Homemade broth keeps well in the refrigerator for up to 5 days. You can keep broth frozen for up to 3 months.

CHICKEN BROTH

This is a basic, inexpensive, and easy recipe you can make with chicken backs, necks, and wings. Or if you like to have boiled chicken around for salads and sandwiches, use a whole chicken. This is an all-purpose broth and can also be used for risotti with meat, vegetables, or seafood. Because this broth is defatted after it is cooled and chilled, it is also suitable to use in the low-fat risotto recipes.

3 to 4 pounds chicken, either whole or in parts

4 large ribs celery, trimmed and cut into 2-inch pieces

3 medium-size carrots, peeled and cut into 2-inch pieces

1 large onion, peeled

1 small bunch fresh parsley, rinsed

2 tablespoons salt

3 quarts cold water

Makes 10 cups

1. COMBINE all the ingredients in a large 8- to 10-quart covered stockpot and place over high heat. When the water comes to a boil, reduce the heat to medium low and partially cover the pot. Cook, skimming the top occasionally, for 1 ½ to 2 hours.

2. STRAIN the broth through a sieve, pressing the meat and vegetables to extract as much liquid as possible. If you like, save the meat and vegetables for another use. Allow the broth to cool, uncovered, to room temperature. Cover securely and refrigerate overnight. Skim the fat from the top of the broth. Transfer to 2 or 3 smaller containers and refrigerate, covered, for up to 5 days or freeze for up to 3 months.

CHINESE CHICKEN BROTH

One 3- to 4-pound whole chicken

⅓ cup sake or other rice wine

Four ¼-inch slices fresh ginger root, unpeeled

1 tablespoon salt

3 quarts cold water

Makes 10 cups

This is a delicately flavored broth to use in any Asian-inspired risotto.

1. COMBINE all the ingredients in a large 8- to 10-quart stockpot, cover, and place over high heat. When the water comes to a boil, reduce the heat to medium low and partially cover. Cook, skimming the top occasionally, for 1 ½ to 2 hours.

2. STRAIN the broth through a sieve, pressing the meat and vegetables to extract as much liquid as possible. Discard the ginger. If you like, save the meat for another use. Allow the broth to cool, uncovered, to room temperature. Cover securely and refrigerate overnight. Skim the fat from the top of the broth. Transfer to 2 or 3 smaller containers and refrigerate, covered, for up to 5 days or freeze for up to 3 months.

SHORTCUT CHINESE CHICKEN BROTH

6 cups canned low-sodium chicken broth

2 cups cold water

2 tablespoons low-sodium soy sauce

Three ¼-inch slices fresh ginger root, unpeeled

Makes 6 cups

COMBINE all the ingredients in a 3- to 4-quart saucepan and place uncovered, over high heat. When the liquid comes to a boil, reduce the heat to medium low and partially cover the pan. Cook 30 minutes. Discard the ginger root pieces, and broth is ready to use.

RICH MEAT BROTH

This is a rich-tasting broth infused with the satisfying, savory flavor of both meat bones and whole chicken. The combination of the two types of meat gives a complexity and dimension of taste that makes risotto particularly delicious.

In Italy, this type of meat broth is the standard broth used in the preparation of most risotto dishes, with the exception of fish and seafood risotto. I would recommend this broth in any recipes calling for meat; if you are not interested in a purely vegetarian dish, it will complement the vegetable risotto as well.

1. COMBINE all the ingredients in a large 8- to 10-quart stockpot, cover, and place over high heat. When the water comes to a boil, reduce the heat to medium low and partially cover the pot. Cook, skimming the top occasionally, for 2 to 3 hours.

2. STRAIN the broth through a sieve, pressing the bones, chicken, and vegetables to extract as much liquid as possible. Discard the bones and reserve the meat and vegetables. Allow the broth to cool, uncovered, to room temperature. Cover securely and refrigerate overnight. Skim the fat from the top of the broth. Transfer to 2 or 3 smaller containers. Refrigerate, covered, for up to 5 days or freeze for up to 3 months.

4 pounds veal and beef bones

2 pounds chicken backs and necks

2 large onions, peeled and coarsely chopped

3 medium-size carrots, peeled and cut into 2-inch pieces

3 large ribs celery, trimmed and cut into 1-inch pieces

1 large leek, white and green parts, cut in half lengthwise, thoroughly rinsed between the layers, and thickly sliced

1 small bunch fresh parsley, rinsed

6 sprigs fresh thyme

2 tablespoons salt

1 teaspoon whole black peppercorns

3 quarts cold water

Makes 10 cups

Basic Vegetable Broth

¼ cup olive oil or other
vegetable oil

1 large onion, peeled and
coarsely chopped

1 large leek, green and white
parts, cut in half lengthwise,
thoroughly rinsed between
the layers to remove sand
and dirt, and thickly sliced

2 medium-size carrots, peeled
and cut into 2-inch pieces

2 ribs celery, trimmed and cut
into 1-inch pieces

2 medium-size turnips, peeled
and coarsely chopped

1 medium-size parsnip, peeled
and cut into 1-inch pieces

2 cups chopped canned
tomatoes, with their juice

1 small bunch fresh parsley,
rinsed

2 tablespoons salt

1 teaspoon whole black
peppercorns

3 quarts cold water

Makes 10 cups

This broth has a light, fresh taste that is suited to most of the vegetarian risotto recipes (see pages 37–65). You can vary the vegetables depending on what you have on hand and what is available. Tomatoes add a lot of flavor so be sure to include them, whether fresh or canned.

1. COMBINE all the ingredients in a large 8- to 10-quart stockpot, cover, and place over high heat. When the water comes to a boil, reduce the heat to medium low and partially cover the pot. Cook, skimming the top occasionally, for 1 ½ hours.

2. STRAIN the broth though a sieve, pressing the vegetables to extract as much liquid as possible. Discard the vegetables. Allow the broth to cool, uncovered, to room temperature. Cover securely and refrigerate overnight. Skim the fat from the top of the broth. Transfer to 2 or 3 smaller containers and refrigerate, covered, for up to 5 days or freeze for up to 3 months.

Roasted Vegetable Broth

I first learned about roasted vegetable broth from Boston chef Andrée Robert. This is an intensely flavorful broth that can be used interchangeably with plain vegetable broth. You can substitute different vegetables and even fruit—pears and apples are wonderful—but try to keep the quantities the same.

1. Preheat the oven to 450 degrees.

2. Pour the oil into a large roasting pan. Add the fresh vegetables, apple, and the salt and toss well to coat with the oil. Place the pan in the oven and roast, stirring once or twice, until the vegetables are just beginning to brown, about 20 minutes.

3. Remove the roasting pan from the oven and transfer the vegetables to a large 8- to 10-quart stockpot. Place the roasting pan over medium-high heat and pour the wine into the pan. Cook, scraping the bottom and sides of the pan with a wooden spoon to loosen any browned bits, until the wine reduces to about ¼ cup, about 3 to 5 minutes.

4. Pour the wine mixture into the stockpot, add the water, tomatoes, parsley, peppercorns, and thyme, and stir to combine. Place the pot, covered, over high heat. When the water comes to a boil, reduce the heat to medium low and partially cover the pot. Cook, skimming the top occasionally, for 1 ½ hours.

5. Strain the broth through a sieve, pressing the vegetables to extract as much liquid as possible. Discard the vegetables. Allow the broth to cool, uncovered, to room temperature. Cover and refrigerate overnight. Skim the fat from the top of the broth. Transfer to 2 or 3 smaller containers and refrigerate for up to 5 days or freeze for up to 3 months.

¼ cup olive oil or other vegetable oil

1 large onion, peeled and coarsely chopped

1 large leek, green and white parts, cut in half lengthwise, thoroughly rinsed between the layers to remove sand and dirt, and thickly sliced

2 medium-size carrots, peeled and cut into 2-inch pieces

2 large ribs celery, rinsed, trimmed, and cut into 1-inch pieces

1 medium-size parsnip, peeled and cut into 1-inch pieces

1 small fennel bulb (about 8 ounces), with top ribs and leaves, cut into 1-inch pieces

2 small red potatoes, scrubbed and sliced

1 Granny Smith apple, cut into wedges

2 tablespoons salt

½ cup dry white wine

3 quarts cold water

2 cups chopped canned tomatoes, with their juice

1 small bunch fresh parsley, rinsed

1 teaspoon whole black peppercorns

6 sprigs fresh thyme

Makes 10 cups

2 to 3 fish frames (about 3 pounds) from nonoily, white-flesh fish

1 large leek, white part only, cut in half lengthwise, thoroughly rinsed between the layers to remove sand and dirt, and thickly sliced

1 large onion, peeled and coarsely chopped

3 medium-size carrots, peeled and coarsely chopped

3 ribs celery, trimmed and coarsely chopped

1 bay leaf

1 heaping teaspoon dried thyme

1 tablespoon salt

1 teaspoon whole black peppercorns

½ cup dry white wine

4 quarts cold water

Makes 3 quarts

The best fish broth is made with the "frames" (the heads with bones and tails attached) of white-fleshed fish such as cod, pollack, sea bass, snapper, flounder, and sole. Use only the freshest frames and avoid frames from oilier fish such as salmon, mackerel, trout, bluefish, tuna, and swordfish as they tend to give a stronger, fishier taste to the broth that is not amenable to the typically delicate taste of seafood risotto. This recipe is adapted from the recipe of my local fish market in Cambridge, The Fishmonger.

1. RINSE the fish frames under cold water to remove any gills or entrails that may remain and place in a large 8- to 10-quart stockpot. Add the vegetables, bay leaf, thyme, salt, and peppercorns. Pour in the wine and water and place, covered, over high heat. When the liquid comes to a boil, reduce the heat to medium low and partially cover the pot. Cook, skimming the top occasionally, for 30 minutes.

2. REMOVE and discard the biggest pieces of bone from the stockpot. Strain the broth through a fine sieve, pressing the bones and vegetables to extract as much liquid as possible. Allow the broth to cool, uncovered, to room temperature. Transfer to 2 or 3 smaller containers and refrigerate for up to 5 days or freeze for up to 3 months. (Discard the sediment that collects on the bottom of the container.)

SHELLFISH BROTH

This flavorful shellfish broth calls for Fish Broth (page 32) and the shells from the shrimp called for in Shrimp and Ginger Risotto (page 71). Use this broth in all the shrimp and lobster risotti. You can keep shrimp shells in the freezer until you accumulate enough to prepare the broth.

1. IN a large 6- to 8-quart pot heat the oil over medium-high heat. Add the onion, shallot, garlic, carrot, celery, fennel, and fennel seeds and cook, stirring, until the vegetables are brown, about 10 minutes.

2. ADD the shrimp shells, wine, tomatoes, parsley, thyme, salt, and peppercorns and continue cooking 10 minutes longer. Add the fish broth and turn the heat to high. When the liquid comes to a boil, partially cover the pot, reduce the heat, and cook, skimming the top occasionally, for 15 minutes. Turn off the heat and allow to stand uncovered, 10 minutes.

3. STRAIN the broth through a fine sieve, pressing on the shells and vegetables to extract as much liquid as possible. Discard the shells and vegetables. Allow the broth to cool, uncovered, to room temperature. Transfer to 2 or 3 smaller containers and refrigerate for up to 5 days or freeze for up to 3 months.

3 tablespoons olive oil or other vegetable oil

1 large onion, peeled and coarsely chopped

1 large shallot, peeled and chopped

2 large cloves garlic, unpeeled, cut in half

1 medium-size carrot, peeled and chopped

2 ribs celery, trimmed and chopped

4 ounces fennel bulb (about one-half small bulb) coarsely chopped

½ teaspoon fennel seeds

Shrimp shells from 8 ounces shrimp, preferably from uncooked shrimp

½ cup dry white wine

1 cup chopped canned tomatoes, with their juice

1 small bunch fresh parsley, rinsed

1 teaspoon dried thyme

1 tablespoon salt

½ teaspoon whole black peppercorns

6 cups fish broth, preferably homemade (page 32); or 5 ½ cups water plus ½ cup clam juice

Makes 1 ½ quarts

chapter FOUR

Vegetable
Risotti

$\mathcal{T}$he tradition of vegetable risotti in Italy is long and strong. Seasonal produce finds its way into the risotto pot, no matter what else is available. And typically, vegetable risotti are simple and uncomplicated, which only serves to enhance the singular flavor of the particular vegetable.

Similarly, fruit—apples, strawberries and lemons—and legumes—beans of all varieties—are also traditional risotto ingredients. In the recipes that follow, traditional and untraditional blend to create new combinations of vegetables for risotto.

Because there is not an established, customary vegetarian cuisine in Italy, vegetable risotti are traditionally prepared there with a meat or chicken broth. Please refer to pages 27–33 for broth recipes and choose the broth you prefer: either a vegetable broth (or even water) to make the recipe vegetarian, or chicken or meat broth for a traditional risotto.

Risotto with Shiitake Mushrooms and Fresh Spinach

Chopped raw spinach instead of the traditional cooked spinach is added to this risotto to make a deliciously fresh-tasting dish. The shiitake mushrooms add heartiness and create a wonderfully satisfying vegetarian main course. Finely chop the spinach in a food processor if you can; it gives the finished dish a uniform, great green color.

1. Heat 2 tablespoons of the oil in a heavy medium-size skillet over medium heat. Add the mushrooms, season with salt to taste, and cook, stirring, until they are tender, 5 to 7 minutes. Turn off the heat and set aside.

2. Combine the remaining tablespoon of oil and 1 tablespoon of the butter in a heavy 4-quart pot over medium-high heat. Add the onion and cook, stirring, until the onion begins to soften, 2 to 3 minutes. Be careful not to brown it. Stir in the rice to coat the grains with the fat and onion mixture, and cook about 1 minute longer.

3. Add the wine and cook, stirring, until it is mostly absorbed by the rice. Add the broth, ½ cup at a time, stirring well after each addition. Wait until each addition is almost completely absorbed before adding the next ½ cup. Reserve ¼ cup to add at the end.

4. When the rice is tender but firm, in about 20 minutes, turn off the heat. Add the remaining ¼ cup broth and 1 tablespoon butter, the cooked mushrooms, spinach, and ½ cup cheese, and stir well to combine with the rice. Season with salt and pepper to taste. Serve immediately. Pass the additional cheese separately.

3 tablespoons olive oil

4 ounces shiitake or other fresh mushrooms, stemmed and sliced (to yield 2 cups)

Salt

2 tablespoons unsalted butter

1 small onion, peeled and finely chopped

2 cups Arborio rice

½ cup dry white wine

6 cups broth of your choice, preferably homemade (pages 27–33), heated

2 cups packed fresh spinach leaves, rinsed, stemmed, dried, and very finely chopped

½ cup freshly grated Italian parmesan cheese, plus additional for serving

Freshly ground black pepper

Makes 4 to 6 servings

WILD MUSHROOM RISOTTO WITH TRUFFLE OIL

1 ounce dried porcini mushrooms (about ⅔ cup
depending on the size of the
porcini pieces)

1 cup water, boiling

3 tablespoons olive oil

1 pound portobello mush-
rooms, stemmed, caps
coarsely chopped (to yield
4 cups)

2 tablespoons unsalted butter

⅓ cup finely chopped shallots

2 cups Arborio rice

½ cup dry white wine

5 cups broth of your choice,
preferably homemade (pages
27–33), heated

½ cup freshly grated Italian
parmesan cheese, plus
additional for serving

2 tablespoons finely chopped
fresh parsley leaves

2 tablespoons truffle oil

Salt

Freshly ground black pepper

Makes 4 to 6 servings

This is the ultimate mushroom risotto with all the best mushroom flavors from dried porcini, fresh portobellos, and the essence of white truffle. Truffle oil is a luxury item. A small 2-ounce bottle will keep for several months in a cool, dark place and is enough to flavor many mushroom risotti. If truffle oil is not available, you can omit it without compromising the recipe.

1. COMBINE the porcini with the boiling water in a heat-proof 2-cup glass measuring cup. Allow to stand at least 15 minutes. Drain the porcini, and chop. Strain the mushroom-soaking liquid through a sieve and combine with the broth.

2. HEAT 2 tablespoons of the olive oil in a heavy medium-size skillet over medium-high heat. Add the portobello mushrooms and cook, stirring, until tender, 5 to 7 minutes. Turn off the heat and set aside.

3. COMBINE the remaining tablespoon of olive oil and 1 tablespoon of the butter in a heavy 4-quart pot over medium-high heat. Add the shallots and cook, stirring, until the shallots begin to soften, 2 to 3 minutes. Be careful not to brown them. Stir in the rice to coat the grains with the butter and shallot mixture, and cook about 1 minute longer.

4. ADD the wine and cook, stirring, until it is mostly absorbed by the rice. Add the drained porcini. Add the broth, ½ cup at a time, stirring well after each addition. Wait until each addition is almost completely absorbed before adding the next ½ cup. Reserve ¼ cup to add at end.

5. WHEN the rice is tender but firm, in about 20 minutes, turn off the heat. Add the remaining ¼ cup broth and 1 tablespoon butter, the cooked portobello mushrooms, ½ cup cheese, parsley, and salt and pepper to taste, and stir well to combine with the rice. Stir in the truffle oil and serve immediately. Pass the additional cheese separately.

6 tablespoons unsalted butter

½ cup finely chopped shallots

2 cups Arborio rice

½ teaspoon pulverized saffron threads (see Box, page 99)

½ cup dry white wine

6 cups broth of your choice, preferably homemade (pages 27–33), heated

½ cup freshly grated Italian parmesan cheese

Salt

Freshly ground black pepper

6 sheets pure 23-carat gold leaf (see Box)

Makes 4 to 6 servings

I was served this extraordinary risotto at the restaurant L'Alberetta, Milanese chef Gualtiero Marchesi's new pavilion to Italian haute cuisine in Erbusco in northern Italy. This is the classic risotto alla milanese, an intensely flavored and vividly orange-colored saffron risotto, made even more dramatic and remarkable than the original because it is served with a small square of pure gold leaf. The steaming risotto gently melts the gold.

1. HEAT 4 tablespoons of the butter in a heavy 4-quart pot over medium-high heat. Add the shallots and cook, stirring, until the shallots gradually soften, 2 to 3 minutes. Be careful not to brown them. Stir in the rice to coat the grains with the butter and shallot mixture, and cook about 1 minute longer.

2. STIR in the saffron; add the wine and cook, stirring, until it is mostly absorbed by the rice. Add the broth, ½ cup at a time, stirring well after each addition. Wait until each addition is almost completely absorbed before adding the next ½ cup. Reserve ¼ cup to add at the end.

3. WHEN the rice is tender but firm, in about 20 minutes, turn off the heat. Add the remaining ¼ cup broth and 2 tablespoons butter, the cheese, and salt and pepper to taste, and stir well to combine with the rice. Serve immediately in individual serving bowls. Top each serving with a sheet of gold leaf.

EDIBLE GOLD

Pure gold leaf—and only if it is 100 percent *pure*—is edible. You can buy 23-carat gold leaf sheets, in what are called "books" of 25 sheets, in fine paint stores. The sheets are about 3 inches square and 3 millionths of an inch thick. Don't use gold alloy sheets; they may contain metals that may be poisonous to ingest.

RISOTTO WITH ZUCCHINI, CHAMPAGNE, AND SQUASH BLOSSOMS

Champagne adds an interesting, distinctive flavor that is different from the customary dry white wine in risotto, and is particularly complemented by the subtle taste of zucchini.

Squash blossoms are listed as optional because they can be difficult to procure unless you grow your own zucchini or have a farmstand nearby that sells them. I am lucky to be able to go to a farmers' market in August where I can buy baby zucchini with the blossoms attached. Squash blossoms are very perishable, so plan to cook them the day you buy or harvest them.

1. COMBINE the oil and 1 tablespoon of the butter in a heavy 4-quart pot over medium-high heat. Add the shallots and cook, stirring, until they begin to soften, 2 to 3 minutes. Be careful not to brown them. Stir in the rice to coat the grains with the oil and shallot mixture, and cook about 1 minute longer.

2. ADD the champagne and cook, stirring, until it is mostly absorbed by the rice. Add the broth, ½ cup at a time, stirring well after each addition. Wait until each addition is almost completely absorbed before adding the next ½ cup. Reserve ¼ cup of the broth to add at the end. After 15 minutes stir in the zucchini and the yellow squash.

3. WHEN the rice is tender but firm, about 5 minutes longer, turn off the heat. Add the remaining ¼ cup broth and 1 tablespoon butter, the zucchini blossoms, cheese, and salt and pepper to taste, and stir well to combine with the rice. Serve immediately. Pass the additional cheese separately.

1 tablespoon olive oil

2 tablespoons unsalted butter

½ cup finely chopped shallots

2 cups Arborio rice

1 cup dry champagne, domestic or French

5 ½ cups broth of your choice, preferably homemade (pages 27–33), heated

1 small zucchini (about 8 ounces), stem end trimmed, diced

1 small yellow summer squash (about 8 ounces), stem end trimmed, diced

6 zucchini blossoms, stamens removed, coarsely chopped, optional

½ cup freshly grated Italian parmesan cheese, plus additional for serving

Salt

Freshly ground black pepper

Makes 4 to 6 servings

Risotto with Artichokes and Watercress

2 medium-size artichokes (about 1 pound total)

2 tablespoons olive oil

1 clove garlic, peeled and pressed or finely chopped

½ cup water

2 tablespoons unsalted butter

1 small onion, peeled and finely chopped

2 cups Arborio rice

½ cup dry white wine

6 cups broth of your choice, preferably homemade (pages 27–33), heated

1 bunch fresh watercress, thickest stems discarded, leaves and remaining stems finely chopped, preferably in a food processor

4 ounces mascarpone cheese (½ cup)

½ cup freshly grated Italian parmesan cheese, plus additional for serving

Salt

Freshly ground black pepper

Makes 4 to 6 servings

This is a delicious risotto with a nice sharp flavor and green color from the watercress. Use fresh artichokes in this recipe. They have a better flavor and texture than frozen artichoke hearts or canned bottoms, which tend to be overcooked and salty.

1. PREPARE the artichokes: Cut the stems, leaving about 1 inch from the base. Pull off the tough, dark green leaves, starting with the leaves closest to the stem, until only the yellow-green leaves are visible. Do not use a scissors or knife for this; the leaves will break naturally at the point where the tough part ends and the tender part begins. Using a serrated knife, cut 2 inches off the top of the artichoke, peel the stem, and trim around the base of the artichoke. Cut the artichoke into quarters lengthwise. Cut out the fuzzy choke from each quarter and the spiky sharp leaves just above it. Thinly slice the artichoke bottoms and chop to yield approximately 2 cups.

2. HEAT 1 tablespoon of the oil with the garlic in a small saucepan over medium heat. Add the chopped artichokes, season with salt to taste, and cook, stirring, about 2 minutes. Add the water to the pan, cover, reduce the heat to low, and cook until the water is evaporated and the artichokes are tender, about 20 minutes. Turn off the heat and set aside.

3. COMBINE the remaining tablespoon of oil and 1 tablespoon of the butter in a heavy 4-quart pot over medium-high heat. Add the onion and cook, stirring, until the onion begins to soften, 2 to 3 minutes. Be careful not to brown it. Stir in the rice to coat the grains with the fat and onion mixture, and cook about 1 minute longer.

4. ADD the wine and cook, stirring, until it is mostly absorbed by the rice. Gradually add the broth, ½ cup at a time, stirring well after each addition. Wait until each addition is almost completely absorbed before adding the next ½ cup. Reserve ¼ cup to add at the end.

5. WHEN the rice is tender but firm, in about 20 minutes, turn off the heat. Add the remaining ¼ cup broth and 1 tablespoon butter, the cooked artichokes, chopped watercress, mascarpone, parmesan, and salt and pepper to taste, and stir well to combine with the rice. Serve immediately. Pass the additional parmesan separately.

PLAN AHEAD

Measure out the ingredients in advance, and chop and cook whatever is called for before you begin to cook the rice. Once you start to prepare risotto you won't have much free-hand time.

Spring Vegetable Risotto

1 tablespoon olive oil

2 tablespoons unsalted butter

½ cup finely chopped onion

¼ cup finely chopped carrot

1 large clove garlic, peeled and
    pressed or finely chopped

2 cups Arborio rice

½ cup dry white wine

6 cups broth of your choice,
    preferably homemade (pages
    27–33), heated

6 thin asparagus spears
    (5 ounces total), tough
    bottoms discarded, spears
    peeled and chopped

1 small zucchini (about 8
    ounces), cut into small dice

½ cup fresh shelled sweet peas
    or defrosted frozen baby
    peas, or use fresh baby fava
    beans (see Box)

½ cup freshly grated Italian
    parmesan cheese, plus
    additional for serving

¼ cup chopped fresh parsley
    leaves, rinsed

Salt

Freshly ground black pepper

Makes 4 to 6 servings

A perfect dish that captures the best flavors of the season, this risotto has a fresh, light taste. If you can find them, baby fava beans are a delicious substitute for the peas. They are available from specialty greengrocers in early spring.

1. COMBINE the oil and 1 tablespoon of the butter in a heavy 4-quart pot over medium-high heat. Add the onion, carrot, and garlic and cook, stirring, until the vegetables begin to soften, 2 to 3 minutes. Be careful not to brown them. Stir in the rice to coat the grains with the fat and vegetable mixture, and cook about 1 minute longer.

2. ADD the wine and cook, stirring, until it is mostly absorbed by the rice. Add the broth, ½ cup at a time, stirring well after each addition. Wait until each addition of broth is almost completely absorbed before adding the next ½ cup. Reserve ¼ cup to add at the end. After 15 minutes add the asparagus, zucchini, and peas.

3. WHEN the rice is tender but firm, about 5 minutes longer, turn off the heat. Add the remaining ¼ cup broth, 1 tablespoon butter, ½ cup cheese, parsley, and salt and pepper to taste. Stir well to combine with the rice. Serve immediately. Pass the additional cheese separately.

FRESH FAVAS

Fava beans are a staple of Italian cooking and particularly popular in southern Italy and Sicily. They are available fresh in the spring and early summer and during the rest of the year, dry. Fresh favas are sold in their pods.

To prepare fresh fava beans, open the pods and remove the beans. The individual beans have a skin that should be peeled off, unless the beans are exceptionally young and small—about the size of a pea. You can lightly steam the favas to remove the skin, or use your fingers to gently press the bean out of its skin.

Asparagus and Pea Risotto with Tarragon

1 tablespoon olive oil

2 tablespoons unsalted butter

½ cup finely chopped shallots

2 cups Arborio rice

½ cup dry white wine

6 cups broth of your choice, preferably homemade (pages 27–33), heated

8 ounces asparagus spears, tough bottoms discarded, spears peeled, chopped

2 tablespoons chopped fresh tarragon leaves

One 10-ounce package frozen peas, defrosted

2 tablespoons mascarpone cheese

½ cup freshly grated Italian parmesan cheese, plus additional for serving

Salt

Freshly ground black pepper

Makes 4 to 6 servings

This is a gloriously green-colored and green-flavored (the asparagus and peas give an intensely fresh taste) risotto inspired by a recipe from L.A. chef Michel Richard.

1. HEAT the oil and 1 tablespoon of the butter in a heavy 4-quart pot over medium-high heat. Add the shallots and cook, stirring, until they begin to soften, 2 to 3 minutes. Be careful not to brown them. Stir in the rice to coat the grains with the butter and shallot mixture, and cook about 1 minute longer.

2. ADD the wine and stir until it is mostly absorbed by the rice. Gradually add the broth, ½ cup at a time, stirring well after each addition. Wait until each addition is almost completely absorbed before adding the next ½ cup. Reserve ¼ cup to add at the end. After 15 minutes stir in the asparagus and the tarragon.

3. WHEN the rice is tender but firm, about 5 minutes longer, turn off the heat.

4. COMBINE the peas and mascarpone in the container of a food processor or blender and purée until smooth and add to the risotto. Stir in the remaining ¼ cup broth, 1 tablespoon butter, ½ cup cheese. Season with salt and pepper to taste. Serve immediately. Pass the additional parmesan separately.

BEET ROOT RISOTTO WITH WILTED WATERCRESS AND GOAT CHEESE

This dish makes a colorful presentation: the bright pink-red beet risotto is served on a bed of wilted leafy greens. You'll find that the risotto has an almost sweet flavor from the beets but it's balanced by the bitter taste of the greens and goat cheese. You can use a good domestic goat cheese. Barely cook the watercress so that it is just wilted.

1. HEAT the butter and 1 tablespoon of the oil in a heavy 4-quart pot over medium-high heat. Add the onion and cook, stirring, until the onion begins to soften, 2 to 3 minutes. Be careful not to brown it. Stir in the rice to coat the grains with the fat and onion mixture, and cook about 1 minute longer.

2. ADD the wine and cook, stirring, until it is mostly absorbed by the rice. Add the beets; begin to add the broth, ½ cup at a time, stirring well after each addition. Wait until each addition is almost completely absorbed before adding the next ½ cup. Reserve ¼ cup to add at the end.

3. WHEN the rice is tender but firm, in about 20 minutes, turn off the heat. Add the remaining ¼ cup broth and the parmesan and stir well until the cheese is combined with the rice. Season with salt and pepper to taste.

4. WORKING quickly, heat the remaining tablespoon of oil in a medium-size skillet over medium-high heat. Add the watercress and cook, stirring, until wilted, 1 to 2 minutes. Arrange the watercress on preheated individual serving plates, spoon some of the risotto over the watercress, and top with the goat cheese. Serve immediately.

1 tablespoon unsalted butter

2 tablespoons olive oil

½ cup finely chopped onion

2 cups Arborio rice

½ cup dry white wine

1 medium-size beet, peeled, top discarded, and grated (to yield about 1 cup)

6 cups broth of your choice, preferably homemade (pages 27–33), heated

½ cup freshly grated Italian parmesan cheese

Salt

Freshly ground black pepper

2 bunches watercress, thickest stems discarded, rinsed, and spun dry

4 ounces unflavored goat cheese, crumbled (about 1 cup crumbled)

Makes 6 servings

Risotto with Fiddlehead Ferns and Gruyère Cheese

8 ounces fiddlehead ferns, stem ends trimmed (see Box)

2 tablespoons unsalted butter

1 tablespoon olive oil

½ cup finely chopped onion

2 cups Arborio rice

½ cup dry white wine

6 cups broth of your choice, preferably homemade (pages 27–33), heated

⅓ cup freshly grated parmesan cheese, plus additional for serving

2 ounces gruyère cheese, chopped or coarsely grated (to yield ½ cup)

Salt

Freshly ground black pepper

Makes 4 to 6 servings

The idea for this risotto comes from the Cambridge restaurant Rialto in the Charles Hotel, where chef Jody Adams prepares this dish with the added gruyère flavoring of smoked bacon or pancetta. I've omitted the bacon/pancetta to make a vegetarian risotto, but you can add bacon or pancetta—2 ounces, diced—with the butter, omitting the oil, in the beginning of the recipe. Cook the bacon until it renders all its fat and becomes brown. Proceed with the directions.

1. PLACE the fiddleheads in a steamer basket over boiling water; cover and steam 5 minutes. Rinse under cold water, drain, and set aside.

2. HEAT 1 tablespoon of the butter with the oil in a heavy 4-quart pot over medium-high heat. Add the onion and cook, stirring, until the onion begins to soften, 2 to 3 minutes. Be careful not to brown it. Stir in the rice to coat the grains with the fat and onion mixture, and cook about 1 minute longer.

3. ADD the wine and cook, stirring, until it is mostly absorbed by the rice. Add the broth, ½ cup at a time, stirring well after each addition. Wait until each addition is almost completely absorbed before adding the next ½ cup. Reserve ¼ cup to add at the end.

4. WHEN the rice is tender but firm, in about 20 minutes, turn off the heat. Add the remaining ¼ cup broth, 1 tablespoon of butter, the steamed fiddleheads, ½ cup parmesan and gruyère cheese, and salt and pepper to taste; stir well to combine with the rice. Serve immediately. Pass the additional parmesan separately.

SELECTING FIDDLEHEADS

When choosing fiddlehead ferns, try to find those that are most tightly coiled and green. As fiddleheads age they uncoil and turn brown.

RISOTTO WITH POTATOES AND BEANS IN A *FRICO* BASKET

FOR THE *FRICO*:

8 ounces grated aged montasio cheese (see Box), or freshly grated parmigiano-reggiano or grana cheese

FOR THE RISOTTO:

1 tablespoon olive oil

2 tablespoons unsalted butter

½ cup finely chopped onion

1 medium-size rib celery, trimmed and finely chopped

2 cups Arborio rice

½ cup dry white wine, preferably a Friulian wine such as Collio or Tocai

1 small boiling potato (about 4 ounces), preferably Yukon Gold, peeled and cut into small dice (to yield 1 cup)

6 cups broth of your choice, preferably homemade (pages 27–33), heated

1 cup cooked small white beans, such as Great Northern or navy beans, rinsed and drained if canned

½ cup freshly grated Italian parmesan cheese, plus additional for serving

In Friuli, the northeasternmost region of Italy, frico, *melted cheese crisps, is a traditional snack. Made with the region's local montasio cheese (you can also use parmigiano-reggiano or grana), the grated cheese is sprinkled into a fry pan and cooked until it is melted and golden brown, then cooled to a crisp. In this recipe, the crisps are cooled over an inverted bowl to give them a basket shape—fanciful vessels for the risotto. You can use frico baskets to serve other vegetable risotti.*

1. PREPARE the *frico*: Have ready a small soup bowl inverted on your work counter next to the stove and a pair of tongs. Place a small, 8-inch skillet with a nonstick surface over medium heat. When the pan is hot, evenly sprinkle ¼ cup of the cheese over the flat surface of the skillet. You don't need to completely cover the surface.

2. WHEN the cheese is melted and bubbling, and beginning to turn golden brown, remove the pan from the heat, and hold it, tilted, over the inverted bowl; use the tongs to gently pull the melted cheese from the pan and lay it flat over the bowl. It should come off in one piece and mold to the form of the bowl. When it is completely cool, remove it from the bowl and set it aside. Repeat with the remaining cheese, to make 6 crisps. The crisps can stand uncovered, at room temperature, for several hours.

3. PREPARE the risotto: Heat the oil with 1 tablespoon of the butter in a heavy 4-quart pot over medium-high heat. Add the onion and celery and cook, stirring, until the vegetables begin to soften, 2 to 3 minutes. Stir in the rice to coat the grains with the fat and onion mixture, and cook about 1 minute longer.

4. ADD the wine and stir until it is mostly absorbed by the rice. Add the potato; begin to add the broth, ½ cup at a time, stirring well after each addition. Wait until each addition is almost completely absorbed before adding the next ½ cup. Reserve ¼ cup to add at the end.

5. WHEN the rice is tender but firm, in about 20 minutes, turn off the heat. Add the remaining ¼ cup broth, 1 tablespoon butter, the beans, ½ cup cheese, parsley, and salt and freshly ground pepper to taste, and stir well until all the ingredients are combined with the rice.

6. TO SERVE, place each *frico* crisp on a warmed dinner plate. Fill with risotto. Top each serving with some of the additional cheese. Serve immediately.

2 tablespoons chopped fresh parsley leaves, rinsed

Salt

Freshly ground black pepper

Makes 4 to 6 servings

MARVELOUS MONTASIO

Montasio is a high-fat cheese made from cow's milk. The younger montasios have a creamy texture and straw color, while the aged cheese is quite firm, almost hard, and has an intense yellow hue. In Friuli, the most popular preparation for aged montasio is the *frico*, melted cheese crisps which are served as a snack or as an antipasto to nibble on with white wine. I think it's also the perfect accompaniment to Friulian risotto. Montasio makes particularly firm *frico*, while parmigiano-reggiano and grana make a more delicate version. *Frico* made from montasio is probably best suited to being formed into a basket shape for serving risotto because it can hold up to the creamy risotto contents. You can serve any risotto in a *frico* basket.

Risotto with Chickpeas, Spinach, and Raisins

2 tablespoons olive oil

½ cup finely chopped onion

2 cloves garlic, peeled and pressed or finely chopped

2 cups Arborio rice

½ cup dry white wine

¼ cup dark raisins

6 cups broth of your choice, preferably homemade (pages 27–33), heated

2 cups packed fresh spinach leaves, rinsed, stemmed, dried, and finely chopped

1 cup cooked chickpeas, rinsed and drained if canned

½ cup freshly grated pecorino romano cheese, or other Italian pecorino grating cheese (see Box)

Grated zest of ½ lemon, about 1 tablespoon

Salt

Freshly ground black pepper

Makes 4 to 6 servings

This risotto is flavored with the tastes of southern Italy and makes a wonderfully flavorful and satisfying dish.

1. HEAT the oil in a heavy 4-quart pot over medium-high heat. Add the onion and garlic and cook, stirring, until the onion begins to soften, 2 to 3 minutes. Be careful not to brown it. Stir in the rice to coat the grains with the oil and onion mixture, and cook about 1 minute longer.

2. ADD the wine and cook, stirring, until it is mostly absorbed by the rice. Add the raisins; begin to add the broth, ½ cup at a time, stirring well after each addition. Wait until each addition is almost completely absorbed before adding the next ½ cup. Reserve ¼ cup to add at the end.

3. WHEN the rice is tender but firm, in about 20 minutes, turn off the heat. Add the remaining ¼ cup broth, spinach, chickpeas, and the cheese, lemon zest, and salt and pepper to taste, and mix well to combine with rice. Serve immediately.

PECORINO CHEESES

Pecorino romano is the most widely available pecorino cheese in the United States. However, it is only one of many pecorino cheeses made in Italy. The regions around Rome, Sardinia, and Sicily are all government-designated areas where the hard pecorino grating cheese is made. Although there are subtle differences among these three pecorini—romano, sardo, and siciliano—they all are made from pure sheep's milk according to traditional methods and share a characteristic aroma, distinctive sharp taste, and hard dry texture that makes them suitable for grating. They can be used interchangeably in recipes calling for pecorino grating cheese. There are other types of pecorino (sheep's milk) cheeses that can be found throughout Italy but are not appropriate for grating.

BLACK BEAN RISOTTO WITH GRILLED VEGETABLES

FOR THE VEGETABLES:

1 medium-size eggplant (about 1 ½ pounds), unpeeled, stem end discarded, and sliced into ½-inch-thick rounds

Salt

1 fennel bulb, trimmed and sliced lengthwise into 6 pieces

2 yellow summer squash (about 8 ounces total), stem ends trimmed, cut in half lengthwise and into thirds crosswise

2 zucchini (about 8 ounces total), stem ends trimmed, cut in half lengthwise and into thirds crosswise

1 large Spanish onion, peeled and sliced into six ¼-inch-thick rounds

Olive oil

FOR THE RISOTTO:

3 tablespoons olive oil

½ cup finely chopped onion

2 cups Arborio rice

½ cup dry white wine

6 cups broth of your choice, preferably homemade (pages 27–33), heated

I enjoyed a risotto very much like this one at the Miami restaurant Bang where former chef Robin Haas prepared many different risotti, all with Caribbean and tropical flavors. If you don't have time to cook the black beans from scratch, use canned beans but rinse them well before adding them to the risotto.

1. PREPARE the vegetables: Light a barbecue grill, or preheat your stove-top grill pan or oven broiler. In a large bowl, combine all the pieces of vegetables with the olive oil and toss until well coated. Grill or broil the vegetables, turning once, until the outsides are brown and the pieces are tender when pierced with a sharp knife, 5 to 7 minutes. The vegetable pieces are large but use a grill basket or grill topper, if you have one, to prevent the vegetables from falling into the fire. Set aside and keep warm until ready to serve.

2. PREPARE the risotto: Heat the oil in a heavy 4-quart pot over medium-high heat. Add the onion and cook, stirring, until the onion begins to soften, 2 to 3 minutes. Be careful not to brown it. Stir in the rice to coat the grains with the oil and onion mixture, and cook about 1 minute longer.

3. ADD the wine and stir until it is mostly absorbed by the rice. Add the broth, ½ cup at a time, stirring well after each addition. Wait until each addition is almost completely absorbed before adding the next ½ cup. Reserve ¼ cup to add at the end.

4. WHEN the rice is tender but firm, in about 20 minutes, turn off the heat. Add the remaining ¼ cup broth, the black beans, ½ cup cheese, and salt and pepper to taste, and stir well until combined with the rice.

5. TO SERVE, spoon the risotto onto warmed dinner plates. Spoon some of the tomato sauce around the perimeter of the risotto. Top with a piece of each of the grilled vegetables. Pass the additional cheese separately.

1 cup cooked black beans, rinsed and drained if canned

½ cup freshly grated Italian parmesan cheese, plus additional for serving

1 cup tomato sauce, preferably homemade, heated

Salt

Freshly ground black pepper

Makes 4 to 6 servings

FINE WINE

When adding wine to risotto, it doesn't need to be heated, but it's best at room temperature.

Risotto with Mustard Greens, Bok Choy, and Tofu

2 tablespoons canola, corn, or other vegetable oil

1 tablespoon finely chopped, peeled fresh ginger root

2 cloves garlic, peeled and pressed or finely chopped

4 scallions, root ends discarded, finely chopped

2 cups American short-grain rice (page 4) or Arborio rice

1 cup chopped bok choy ribs, white parts only

¼ cup rice wine (sake)

6 cups Chinese Chicken Broth (page 28) or broth of your choice, preferably home-made (pages 27–33), heated

2 cups finely chopped mustard greens

4 ounces firm tofu, diced

1 tablespoon soy sauce

1 tablespoon hot chili-flavored sesame oil (see Note)

Makes 4 to 6 servings

Note:
Flavored oils are available in specialty food shops and Asian markets.

The idea of Chinese risotto comes from Yujean Kang, a chef and restaurateur in Pasadena, California. For this risotto you can use American short-grain rice which is sold in Asian markets as Nishiki or Chinese rice.

1. HEAT the oil in a heavy 4-quart pot over medium-high heat. Add the ginger, garlic, and half the scallion and cook, stirring, until the scallion begins to soften, about 2 minutes. Stir in the rice to coat the grains with the oil and seasonings, and cook about 1 minute longer. Add the bok choy and stir to combine.

2. ADD the rice wine and cook, stirring, until it is mostly absorbed by the rice. Add the broth, ½ cup at a time, stirring well after each addition. Wait until each addition is almost completely absorbed before adding the next ½ cup. Reserve ¼ cup to add at the end.

3. WHEN the rice is tender but firm, in about 20 minutes, turn off the heat. Add the reserved broth, the mustard greens, tofu, and soy sauce and stir well to combine. Drizzle some of the chili oil over each serving. Garnish with the remaining scallions. Serve immediately.

Risotto with Pan-Roasted Eggplant and Mozzarella

This is a rustic risotto with hearty flavors.

1. Put the eggplant in a large colander, sprinkle it liberally with salt, and allow to stand and drain 30 minutes.

2. Heat 1 tablespoon of the oil in a medium-size heavy skillet over medium-high heat. Add the eggplant and red pepper flakes and cook, stirring almost constantly, until the eggplant is brown and tender when pierced with a sharp knife, about 5 minutes. Turn off the heat, stir in the garlic, and set aside.

3. Heat 2 tablespoons of the oil in a heavy 4-quart pot over medium-high heat. Add the onion and cook, stirring, until the onion begins to soften, 2 to 3 minutes. Be careful not to brown it. Stir in the rice to coat the grains with the oil and onion mixture, and cook about 1 minute longer.

4. Add the wine and stir until it is mostly absorbed by the rice. Add the tomatoes; begin to add the broth, ½ cup at a time, stirring well after each addition. Wait until each addition is almost completely absorbed before adding the next ½ cup. Reserve ¼ cup to add at the end.

5. When the rice is tender but firm, in about 20 minutes, turn off the heat. Add the remaining ¼ cup broth, the eggplant, mozzarella, ⅓ cup parmesan, parsley, basil, and salt and pepper to taste, and stir well to combine with the rice. Serve immediately. Pass the additional parmesan separately.

1 small eggplant (about 1 pound), unpeeled, stem end discarded, and cut into ½-inch dice (to yield 4 cups)

Salt

3 tablespoons olive oil

Pinch red pepper flakes

1 clove garlic, peeled and pressed or finely chopped

½ cup finely chopped onion

2 cups Arborio rice

½ cup dry white wine

½ cup chopped canned tomatoes, with their juice

6 cups broth of your choice, preferably homemade (pages 27–33), heated

4 ounces whole-milk mozzarella cheese, cut into small cubes

⅓ cup freshly grated Italian parmesan cheese, plus additional for serving

¼ cup chopped fresh parsley leaves, rinsed

2 tablespoons chopped fresh basil leaves

Freshly ground black pepper

Makes 4 to 6 servings

Parmesan Risotto and Eggplant Ragout

FOR THE RAGOUT:

1 small eggplant (about 1 pound), unpeeled, stem end discarded, and cut into ½-inch cubes

Salt

2 tablespoons olive oil

½ cup chopped onion

3 cloves garlic, peeled and finely chopped

1 small zucchini (about 8 ounces), stem end discarded, cubed

4 ounces fresh fennel bulb, coarsely chopped

1 small red bell pepper, cored, seeded, and diced

6 plum tomatoes (about 1 pound total), peeled, seeded, and chopped

1 tablespoon fresh oregano leaves or 1 teaspoon dried

½ cup cold water

2 tablespoons chopped fresh parsley leaves, rinsed

3 tablespoons chopped fresh basil leaves

FOR THE RISOTTO:

2 tablespoons olive oil

½ cup finely chopped onion

2 cups Arborio rice

A classic way to serve risotto in Italy is with a stew, ragù, or sauce over a simple, cheese risotto. You can prepare the eggplant ragout in advance and reheat it to serve with the risotto.

1. PREPARE the ragout: Place the eggplant in a large colander, sprinkle it liberally with salt, and allow to stand and drain 30 minutes.

2. HEAT the oil in a large saucepan with a tight-fitting lid over medium heat. Add the onion and garlic and cook until the onion is translucent, 5 to 7 minutes. Add the salted eggplant, zucchini, fennel, red pepper, tomatoes, and oregano and stir to combine. Cook, uncovered, until the vegetables begin to soften, 2 to 3 minutes. Add the water, cover the saucepan, and simmer over medium-low heat for 15 minutes. Stir in the parsley and basil; turn off the heat and set aside.

3. PREPARE the risotto: Heat the oil in a heavy 4-quart pot over medium-high heat. Add the onion and cook, stirring, until the onion begins to soften, 2 to 3 minutes. Be careful not to brown it. Stir in the rice to coat the grains with the oil and onion mixture, and cook about 1 minute longer.

4. ADD the wine and stir until it is mostly absorbed by the rice. Add the broth, ½ cup at a time, stirring well after each addition. Wait until each addition is almost completely absorbed before adding the next ½ cup. Reserve ¼ cup to add at the end.

5. WHEN the rice is tender but firm, in about 20 minutes, turn off the heat. Add the remaining ¼ cup broth, ¾ cup cheese, and salt and pepper to taste, and stir to combine.

6. TO SERVE, spoon the risotto onto warmed dinner plates. Top with some of the eggplant ragout. Pass the additional cheese separately.

½ cup dry white wine

6 cups broth of your choice, preferably homemade (pages 27–33), heated

¾ cup freshly grated Italian parmesan cheese, plus additional for serving

Freshly ground black pepper

Makes 4 to 6 servings

NONSTICK RISOTTO

It's okay to use a pot with a nonstick surface, provided it's a good heavy pot that meets the qualifications of a good risotto pot (see page 8). A nonstick pot makes the cleanup a whole lot faster and easier.

APPLE RISOTTO WITH CURRANTS

2 tablespoons unsalted butter

1 medium-size Granny Smith
   apple, cut into quarters,
   peeled, cored, and diced

½ cup dried currants

2 tablespoons olive oil

½ cup finely chopped onion

2 cups Arborio rice

½ cup dry white wine

6 cups broth of your choice,
   preferably homemade (pages
   27–33), heated

⅓ cup freshly grated Italian
   parmesan cheese

Salt

Freshly ground black pepper

   Makes 4 to 6 servings

*With just a hint of sweetness, this apple risotto has a great com-
forting fall taste. You can use Granny Smith or yellow Delicious
apples any time of year to prepare this recipe. Even better, use
fresh-picked fall apples that are tart and crunchy, if you can get
them. Serve this risotto as an accompaniment to roast pork or
grilled chicken paillard.*

1. HEAT 1 tablespoon of the butter in a small skillet over
   medium heat. Add the apple and the currants and cook,
   stirring, until the apple begins to soften, about 5 minutes. Turn off the heat and set aside.

2. HEAT the remaining butter with the oil in a heavy
   4-quart pot over medium-high heat. Add the onion and
   cook, stirring, until the onion begins to soften, 2 to 3
   minutes. Be careful not to brown it. Stir in the rice to
   coat the grains with the fat and onion mixture, and cook
   about 1 minute longer

3. ADD the wine and stir until it is mostly absorbed by the
   rice. Add the broth, ½ cup at a time, stirring well after
   each addition. Wait until each addition is almost completely absorbed before adding the next ½ cup. Reserve
   ¼ cup to add at the end.

4. WHEN the rice is tender but firm, in about 20 minutes,
   turn off the heat. Add the remaining ¼ cup broth, the
   apple and currant mixture, cheese, and salt and pepper
   to taste, and stir well to combine with the rice. Serve
   immediately.

Risotto with Spaghetti Squash, Fresh Tomatoes, Basil, and Fontina

This dish is one of the best ways I've found to enjoy the stringy-fleshed spaghetti squash. You can steam the squash, but roasting gives it a more robust, rich flavor that enhances the risotto.

1. PREHEAT the oven to 400 degrees.

2. PLACE the squash, cut side up, in a small baking pan, brush with 1 tablespoon of the olive oil, and season with salt and pepper to taste. Place on the top shelf in the oven and roast until tender when pierced with a sharp knife, 40 to 45 minutes.

3. REMOVE the squash from the oven, allow to cool slightly, and use a spoon to scoop the squash from its skin. Coarsely chop the squash to yield 3 cups.

4. HEAT the remaining oil in a heavy 4-quart pot over medium-high heat. Add the onion and garlic and cook, stirring, until the onion begins to soften, 2 to 3 minutes. Be careful not to brown it. Stir in the rice to coat the grains with the oil and onion mixture, and cook about 1 minute longer.

5. ADD the wine and stir until it is mostly absorbed by the rice. Add the broth, ½ cup at a time, stirring well after each addition. Wait until each addition is almost completely absorbed before adding the next ½ cup. Reserve ¼ cup to add at the end.

6. WHEN the rice is tender but firm, in about 20 minutes, turn off the heat. Add the remaining ¼ cup broth, the squash, tomatoes, basil, ½ cup parmesan, fontina, and salt and pepper to taste, and stir well to combine with the rice. Serve immediately. Pass the additional parmesan separately.

1 small spaghetti squash (about 2 pounds), cut in half lengthwise and seeded

3 tablespoons olive oil

Salt

Freshly ground black pepper

½ cup finely chopped onion

2 cloves garlic, peeled and pressed or finely chopped

2 cups Arborio rice

½ cup dry white wine

6 cups broth of your choice, preferably homemade (pages 27–33), heated

6 small plum tomatoes (about 1 pound total), seeded and chopped (to yield ¾ cup)

½ cup shredded fresh basil leaves

½ cup freshly grated Italian parmesan cheese, plus additional for serving

3 ounces Italian fontina cheese, rind removed, cut into 1-inch cubes (to yield 1 cup, loosely packed)

Makes 4 to 6 servings

Risotto with Sweet Peppers, Papaya, and Citrus

3 tablespoons canola, corn, or
other vegetable oil

½ cup seeded and diced green
bell pepper

½ cup seeded and diced yellow
bell pepper

½ cup seeded and diced red bell
pepper

2 large cloves garlic, peeled and
pressed or finely chopped

One 1-pound papaya, peeled,
seeded, and diced (to yield
2 cups)

1 lime, zest grated, juiced (to
yield 2 tablespoons lime
juice)

½ cup finely chopped onion

2 cups Arborio rice

½ cup dry white wine

6 cups broth of your choice,
preferably homemade (pages
27–33), heated

¼ cup chopped fresh cilantro
leaves

2 ounces coarsely grated
Monterey Jack cheese

½ teaspoon Tabasco sauce or
more to taste

Salt

Freshly ground black pepper

Makes 4 to 6 servings

This is a colorful and highly flavored risotto that has the verve, vitality, and tastes associated with the tropics. Papaya in risotto may seem far out, but there is a tradition of fruit risotti in Italy, including such classics as strawberry risotto and citrus risotto. The fruit in this dish doesn't add sweetness, it just adds flavor. Serve this risotto as an accompaniment to grilled fish.

1. HEAT 1 tablespoon of the oil in a medium-size skillet over medium heat. Add the peppers and cook, stirring, until they begin to soften, 2 to 3 minutes. Turn off the heat. Stir in the garlic, papaya, and the grated lime zest and set aside.

2. HEAT the remaining 2 tablespoons of oil in a heavy 4-quart pot over medium-high heat. Add the onion and cook, stirring, until the onion begins to soften, 2 to 3 minutes. Be careful not to brown it. Stir in the rice to coat the grains with the oil and onion mixture, and cook about 1 minute longer

3. ADD the wine and stir until it is mostly absorbed by the rice. Add the broth, ½ cup at a time, stirring well after each addition. Wait until each addition is almost completely absorbed before adding the next ½ cup. Reserve ¼ cup to add at the end.

4. WHEN the rice is tender but firm, in about 20 minutes, turn off the heat. Add the remaining ¼ cup broth, the pepper and papaya mixture, lime juice, cilantro, cheese, Tabasco, and salt and pepper to taste, and stir well to combine. Serve immediately.

SOFRITO AND CORN RISOTTO

This recipe comes from Steven Raichlen, a food writer who lives in Miami. Steven recommends using corn from barbecue-grilled ears, but any corn kernels work in this South Florida–style Italian dish. Sofrito *is the Spanish word for the onion, pepper, and garlic mixture.*

1. HEAT the oil in a heavy 4-quart pot over medium-high heat. Add the onion, red pepper, corn, and garlic and cook, stirring, until the onion begins to soften, 2 to 3 minutes. Stir in the rice to coat the grains with the oil and vegetable mixture, and cook about 1 minute longer.

2. ADD the wine and stir until it is mostly absorbed by the rice. Add the broth, ½ cup at a time, stirring well after each addition. Wait until each addition is almost completely absorbed before adding the next ½ cup. Reserve ¼ cup to add at the end.

3. WHEN the rice is tender but firm, in about 20 minutes, turn off the heat. Add the reserved broth, ½ cup cheese, and parsley, and stir well until combined with the rice. Season with salt and pepper to taste. Serve immediately. Pass the additional cheese separately.

2 tablespoons olive oil

½ cup finely chopped onion

1 medium-size red bell pepper, cored, seeded, and cut into small dice

1 cup cooked corn kernels, preferably cut from barbecue-grilled corn ears, or boiled or defrosted, frozen corn

2 cloves garlic, peeled and finely chopped or pressed

2 cups Arborio rice

½ cup dry white wine

6 cups broth of your choice, preferably homemade (pages 27–33), heated

½ cup freshly grated Italian parmesan cheese, plus additional for serving

¼ cup chopped fresh parsley leaves, rinsed

Salt

Freshly ground black pepper

Makes 4 to 6 servings

Risotto with Curried Cauliflower, Lentils, and Nectarine Chutney

FOR THE CHUTNEY:

1 teaspoon olive oil

½ cup chopped red onion

2 teaspoons finely chopped, peeled fresh ginger root

1 clove garlic, peeled and pressed or finely chopped

1 nectarine, seeded and chopped

2 heaping teaspoons packed dark brown sugar

½ teaspoon ground cumin

Pinch ground coriander

3 tablespoons red wine vinegar

¼ cup golden raisins

2 tablespoons water

Salt

Freshly ground black pepper

FOR THE RISOTTO:

3 tablespoons olive oil

1 cup finely chopped onion

1 clove garlic, peeled and pressed or finely chopped

1 teaspoon finely chopped, peeled fresh ginger root

½ head cauliflower, cut into small florets (to yield 2 cups)

Curry is a popular ingredient in Italian cooking although few people associate it with Italy. In this vegetarian risotto the flavors of Italy and India blend harmoniously.

1. PREPARE the chutney: Heat the oil in a small saucepan over medium heat. Add the onion, ginger, and garlic and cook, stirring, until the onion begins to soften, 2 to 3 minutes. Stir in the nectarine, brown sugar, cumin, coriander, vinegar, raisins, water, and salt and pepper to taste. Bring to a boil, reduce the heat to medium low, and simmer, partially covered, for 10 minutes. Transfer to a serving dish and cool to room temperature before serving.

2. PREPARE the risotto: Heat 1 tablespoon of the oil in a small saucepan over medium heat. Add ½ cup of the onion, garlic, and ginger and cook, stirring, until the onion begins to soften, 2 to 3 minutes. Add the cauliflower, lentils, curry powder, fennel seeds, cardamom, coriander; season with salt to taste. Stir in 1 cup of the broth and bring the liquid to a boil. Reduce the heat to low. Cover and cook until the lentils are tender, 25 to 30 minutes.

3. HEAT the remaining 2 tablespoon of oil in a heavy 4-quart pot over medium-high heat. Add the remaining ½ cup of the onion and cook, stirring, until the onion begins to soften, 2 to 3 minutes. Be careful not to brown it. Stir in the rice to coat the grains with the oil and onion mixture, and cook about 1 minute longer

4. ADD the remaining broth, ½ cup at a time, stirring well after each addition. Wait until each addition of broth is almost completely absorbed before adding the next ½ cup.

5. WHEN the rice is tender but firm, in about 20 minutes, turn off the heat. Add the cauliflower mixture and stir well to combine with the rice. Season to taste with salt and pepper. Serve immediately. Pass the chutney separately.

2 tablespoons brown lentils

1 teaspoon curry powder

Pinch fennel seeds

Pinch ground cardamom

¼ teaspoon ground coriander

7 cups broth of your choice, preferably homemade (pages 27–33), heated

2 cups Arborio rice

Salt

Freshly ground black pepper

Makes 4 to 6 servings

MORE BROTH

To determine when it's time to add more broth to your risotto, run your wooden spoon across the bottom of the pot; your spoon should be able to create a clear wake behind the spoon.

chapter FIVE

Seafood and Fish Risotti

With so much of Italian coastline bordering on the Mediterranean and the Adriatic seas, and the regions of northern Italy inundated with rivers and lakes, there is a wealth of great fresh and saltwater fish and seafood risotti throughout Italy. Most of the recipes that follow are contemporary versions of traditional Italian preparations. All the recipes call for American fish and seafood that is available in most of our better or bigger fish markets.

In keeping with Italian custom, you will not find cheese in these fish and seafood risotti: fish and cheese don't mix in Italian cooking in pasta, soups, or risotto. The flavors compete, according to Italian cooks. Cheese, therefore, is not in the risotto, and it's not served with the risotto at the table.

But when it comes to broth, the rules are not so strict. Fish broth and chicken broth can be used interchangeably—with some cooks using only fish broth for fish risotto while others swear the best taste can only come from a good homemade *brodo di gallina*, chicken broth. In the following recipes you will find a mixture: Some recipes call for fish broth; others for chicken or shrimp broth—all depending on what I found tastes best for each risotto.

CRAB AND ASPARAGUS RISOTTO

Asparagus and crab meat combine to make a delicious risotto. Use fresh, unfrozen, lump crab meat and delicate thin asparagus spears for the best results.

1. HEAT the olive oil and 1 tablespoon of the butter in a heavy 4-quart pot over medium-high heat. Add the onion and garlic and cook, stirring, until the onion begins to soften, 2 to 3 minutes. Be careful not to brown it. Stir in the rice to coat the grains with the fat and onion mixture, and cook about 1 minute longer.

2. ADD the wine and stir until it is mostly absorbed by the rice. Add the broth, ½ cup at a time, stirring well after each addition. Wait until each addition is almost completely absorbed by the rice before adding the next ½ cup. Reserve ¼ cup of broth to add at the end. After 15 minutes stir in the asparagus.

3. WHEN the rice is tender but firm, about 5 minutes longer, turn off the heat. Add the remaining ¼ cup broth and 1 tablespoon butter, the crab meat, parsley, and salt and pepper to taste, and stir well to combine with the rice. Serve immediately.

1 tablespoon olive oil

2 tablespoons unsalted butter

½ cup finely chopped onion

1 clove garlic, peeled and pressed or finely chopped

2 cups Arborio rice

½ cup dry white wine

6 cups fish broth, preferably homemade (page 32), heated

1 pound thin asparagus spears, tough bottoms discarded, spears peeled and chopped (to yield 2 cups)

8 ounces fresh crab meat, picked over to remove any pieces of shell

¼ cup chopped fresh parsley leaves, rinsed

Salt

Freshly ground black pepper

Makes 4 to 6 servings

Risotto with Crab Meat, Butternut Squash, and Gremolada

2 tablespoons unsalted butter

1 tablespoon olive oil

½ cup finely chopped shallots

2 cups Arborio rice

½ cup dry white wine

1 cup grated, peeled butternut squash

6 cups fish broth, preferably homemade (page 32), heated

8 ounces cooked crab meat, picked over to remove any pieces of shell

1 tablespoon grated or finely chopped lemon zest

2 tablespoons chopped fresh parsley leaves, rinsed

1 clove garlic, peeled and pressed or finely chopped

Salt

Freshly ground black pepper

Makes 4 to 6 servings

On Italy's eastern coast, shore crabs from the Adriatic Sea are often cooked in risotto. I like to use the sweet Maine crab meat we get in the Northeast where I live, but you should use whatever crab meat is available in your area and add it just when the risotto is finished cooking. Be careful not to overcook; crab meat is already cooked and the delicate taste needs only to be warmed through. Gremolada is a mixture of lemon, garlic, and parsley and adds just the right amount of zest to this ever-so-subtly flavored dish. Crab risotto makes wonderful risotto cakes, see pages 174–75.

1. HEAT 1 tablespoon of the butter with the oil in a heavy 4-quart pot over medium-high heat. Add the shallots and cook, stirring, until the shallots begin to soften, 2 to 3 minutes. Be careful not to brown them. Stir in the rice to coat the grains with the butter, oil, and shallot mixture, and cook about 1 minute longer.

2. ADD the wine and stir until it is mostly absorbed by the rice. Add the butternut squash; begin to add the broth, ½ cup at a time, stirring well after each addition. Wait until each addition is almost completely absorbed by the rice before adding the next ½ cup. Reserve ¼ cup of broth to add at the end.

3. WHEN the rice is tender but firm, in about 20 minutes, turn off the heat. Add the remaining ¼ cup broth and 1 tablespoon butter, the crab, lemon zest, parsley, garlic, and salt and pepper to taste, and stir well to combine with the rice. Serve immediately.

SHRIMP AND GINGER RISOTTO

This dish was inspired by a wonderful langoustine (crustaceans that resemble crayfish, which are native to Western Europe) risotto I tasted at Rex Il Ristorante, an elegant, classic Italian restaurant in Los Angeles owned by Mauro and Maureen Vincente. Their chef prepared three risotti in my honor. This risotto gets extra flavor from a rich shellfish broth.

1. HEAT 1 tablespoon of the butter and oil in a heavy 4-quart saucepan over medium-high heat. Add the ginger and onion and cook, stirring, until the onion begins to soften, 2 to 3 minutes. Be careful not to brown it. Stir in the rice to coat the grains with the fat and onion mixture, and cook about 1 minute longer.

2. ADD the wine and stir until it is mostly absorbed by the rice. Add the broth, ½ cup at a time, stirring well after each addition. Wait until each addition is almost completely absorbed before adding the next ½ cup. Reserve ¼ cup of broth to add at the end. When the risotto has been cooking 15 minutes, add the shrimp.

3. WHEN the rice is tender but firm, about 5 minutes longer, turn off the heat. Add the remaining ¼ cup broth, 2 tablespoons of butter, and the parsley and stir well to combine with the rice. Season with salt and pepper to taste. Serve immediately.

3 tablespoons unsalted butter

2 tablespoons olive oil

1 tablespoon finely chopped, peeled fresh ginger root

½ cup chopped onion

2 cups Arborio rice

⅔ cup dry white wine

6 cups Shellfish Broth (page 33), heated

1 pound medium-size raw shrimp, peeled (shells reserved), deveined, and coarsely chopped (to yield 1 cup)

¼ cup chopped fresh parsley leaves, rinsed

Salt

Freshly ground black pepper

Makes 4 to 6 servings

STEADY SIMMER

Keep the risotto cooking at an even, lively but low boil. If the heat is too high, the liquid evaporates too quickly, and the rice sticks and browns in the pot. If the heat is too low, the broth is not absorbed quickly enough, the rice grains lose their firmness, and the risotto does not have the desired consistency.

Risotto with Tomatoes and Spicy Grilled Shrimp

FOR THE SHRIMP:

1 pound medium-size raw
    shrimp, peeled and deveined

1 tablespoon olive oil

2 cloves garlic, peeled and
    pressed or finely chopped

Juice of ½ lemon (about
    2 tablespoons)

½ teaspoon red pepper flakes,
    or more to taste

Salt

Freshly ground black pepper

FOR THE RISOTTO:

1 tablespoon olive oil

2 tablespoons unsalted butter

½ cup finely chopped onion

2 cups Arborio rice

1 cup chopped canned
    tomatoes, with their juice

5 cups chicken broth,
    preferably homemade
    (pages 27–28), heated

2 tablespoons chopped fresh
    parsley leaves, rinsed

2 tablespoons chopped fresh
    basil leaves

Salt

Freshly ground black pepper

Makes 4 to 6 servings

1. PREPARE the shrimp: In a small, nonreactive mixing bowl, combine the shrimp with the oil, garlic, lemon juice, red pepper flakes, and salt and pepper to taste; toss to mix. Allow to stand at room temperature at least 1 hour, or refrigerate until ready to cook.

2. LIGHT the barbecue grill, or preheat a stove-top grill pan or oven broiler.

3. PREPARE the risotto: Heat the olive oil with 1 tablespoon of the butter in a heavy 4-quart pot over medium-high heat. Add the onion and cook, stirring, until the onion begins to soften, 2 to 3 minutes. Be careful not to brown it. Stir in the rice to coat the grains with the oil and onion mixture, and cook about 1 minute longer.

4. ADD the tomatoes and begin to add the broth, ½ cup at a time, stirring well after each addition. Wait until each addition of broth is almost completely absorbed before adding the next ½ cup. Reserve ¼ cup of broth to add at the end.

5. WHILE the risotto is cooking, grill the shrimp, about 3 minutes on a side. (If you're using a barbecue, you may want to skewer the shrimp or use a seafood tray to keep the shrimp from falling through the grates.)

6. WHEN the rice is tender but firm, in about 20 minutes, turn off the heat. Add the remaining ¼ cup broth and 1 tablespoon butter, the parsley, basil, and salt and pepper to taste, and stir well to combine with the rice. Spoon the risotto into warmed individual bowls. Top each serving with some of the shrimp. Serve immediately.

RISOTTO WITH SHRIMP AND COCONUT MILK

This is a pungent dish with wonderful flavors, great aromas, and a soothing, pale pink, tropical color. This recipe comes from Boston chef Didi Emmons, who prepares it at the Delux Cafe.

1. COMBINE the shrimp shells with the broth in a small saucepan over medium heat. Cook for 10 minutes. Strain the broth and return it to the saucepan. Reheat the broth before adding it to the risotto. Discard the shells.

2. HEAT the oil in a heavy 4-quart pot over medium-high heat. Add the onion, garlic, fennel seed, and red pepper flakes; cook, stirring, until the onion begins to soften, 2 to 3 minutes. Be careful not to brown it. Stir in the rice to coat the grains with the oil and onion mixture, and cook about 1 minute longer.

3. ADD the wine, tarragon, and tomatoes and stir until the wine is mostly absorbed by the rice. Add the coconut milk and continue to cook, stirring, until the milk is mostly absorbed by the rice. Add the broth, ½ cup at a time, stirring well after each addition. Wait until each addition is almost completely absorbed before adding the next ½ cup. Reserve ¼ cup of broth to add at the end. When the rice has been cooking 15 minutes, add the shrimp.

4. WHEN the rice is tender but firm, about 5 minutes longer, turn off the heat. Add the remaining ¼ cup broth, the scallion, lime juice, and salt and pepper to taste. Serve immediately.

Note:
Coconut milk is available in Asian and Caribbean markets.

8 ounces small raw shrimp, peeled (shells reserved) and deveined

5 cups chicken broth, preferably homemade (pages 27–28), heated

2 tablespoons canola, corn, or other vegetable oil

1 cup finely chopped onion

2 large cloves garlic, peeled and pressed or finely chopped

½ teaspoon fennel seed

Pinch red pepper flakes or chopped hot red pepper, seeded

2 cups Arborio rice

½ cup dry white wine

1 teaspoon dried tarragon leaves

2 small plum tomatoes, peeled, seeded, and chopped; or ¼ cup canned tomatoes, drained and chopped

1 cup unsweetened coconut milk (see Note)

¼ cup chopped scallion greens

Juice of 1 lime (about 2 tablespoons)

Salt

Freshly ground black pepper

Makes 4 to 6 servings

RISOTTO WITH SHRIMP AND BLACK BEAN SAUCE

FOR THE RISOTTO:

2 tablespoons canola, corn, or other vegetable oil

2 tablespoons finely chopped whole scallions

1 tablespoon finely chopped, peeled fresh ginger root

2 large cloves garlic, peeled and pressed or finely chopped

1 ½ cups American short-grain rice (page 4) or Arborio rice

½ cup rice wine (sake)

6 cups Chinese Chicken Broth (page 28) or Shortcut Chinese Chicken Broth (page 28), heated

1 cup chopped, peeled broccoli stems

1 cup roughly chopped bok choy

FOR THE SHRIMP:

1 tablespoon canola, corn, or other vegetable oil

4 scallions, root ends discarded, white part finely chopped, green tops chopped and kept separate

This savory risotto is seasoned with traditional Chinese ingredients. The recipe calls for broccoli stems, which often get discarded but are worth saving. They are a wonderful addition for both tang and texture in this dish.

1. PREPARE the risotto: Heat the oil in a 4-quart heavy pot over medium-high heat. Add the scallion, ginger, and garlic and cook, stirring, until the scallion begins to soften, 1 to 2 minutes. Stir in the rice to coat the grains with the oil and seasonings, and cook about 1 minute longer.

2. ADD the rice wine and stir until the wine has mostly been absorbed by the rice. Add the broth, ½ cup at a time, stirring well after each addition. Wait until each addition of broth is almost completely absorbed before adding the next ½ cup. Reserve ¼ cup of broth to add at the end. After 15 minutes add the broccoli and the bok choy.

3. PREPARE the shrimp while the rice is cooking: Heat the oil in a small heavy skillet over medium heat. Add the scallion whites, garlic, and ginger and cook, stirring, until the scallion begins to soften, 1 to 2 minutes. Stir in the shrimp and the pepper flakes and cook, stirring, until the shrimp begins to turn pink, 1 to 2 minutes longer. Add the black bean paste and the broth and stir well to combine. Continue to cook the shrimp until the sauce has thickened slightly and the shrimp is cooked through, 5 to 7 minutes. Turn off the heat and set aside.

4. WHEN the rice is tender but firm, after 20 minutes, turn off the heat. Add the remaining ¼ cup broth and salt and pepper to taste, and stir well to combine with the rice.

5. TO SERVE, spoon the risotto into warmed individual serving bowls. Top with the shrimp and black bean sauce and garnish with the scallion greens. Serve immediately.

HOT BROTH

Always add very hot or barely simmering broth to the rice. This helps to maintain an even cooking temperature.

2 large cloves garlic, peeled and pressed or finely chopped

2 tablespoons finely chopped, peeled fresh ginger root

1 pound small raw shrimp, peeled (shells reserved) and deveined

Pinch red pepper flakes

2 tablespoons prepared black bean paste (see Note)

½ cup Chinese Chicken Broth (page 28) or Shortcut Chinese Chicken Broth (page 28), heated

Salt

Freshly ground black pepper

Makes 4 to 6 servings

Note:
Prepared black bean paste is available in some well-stocked supermarkets and all Asian markets.

BUTTERY RISOTTO WITH SEARED SCALLOPS AND SPINACH

18 whole spinach leaves, rinsed, stemmed, and dried

4 tablespoons unsalted butter

½ cup finely chopped onion

2 cups Arborio rice

½ cup dry white wine

6 cups chicken broth, preferably homemade (page 27–28), heated

3 tablespoons canola, corn, or other vegetable oil

18 large sea scallops (about 1 pound total)

Salt

Freshly cracked black peppercorns

Makes 4 to 6 servings

This dish takes a plain butter risotto and transforms it into a sumptuous, striking dish. The steamed spinach leaves are arranged on the crown of the risotto and embellished with seared scallops on the top.

Use the large sea scallops in this dish and figure three for each serving. Cook the scallops while you prepare the risotto.

1. PLACE the spinach leaves in a steamer basket over boiling water, cover, and steam 3 minutes. Remove to a large plate or piece of wax paper, keeping them intact and whole as much as possible, cover with plastic wrap to keep warm and set aside until ready to serve.

2. HEAT 2 tablespoons of the butter in a heavy 4-quart pot over medium-high heat. Add the onion and cook, stirring, until it begins to soften, 2 to 3 minutes. Be careful not to brown it. Stir in the rice to coat the grains with the butter and onion mixture, and cook about 1 minute longer.

3. ADD the wine and stir until it is mostly absorbed by the rice. Add the broth, ½ cup at a time, stirring well after each addition. Wait until each addition is almost completely absorbed before adding the next ½ cup. Reserve ¼ cup of broth to add at the end.

4. WHILE the rice is cooking, prepare the scallops: Heat the oil in a small skillet over medium-high heat until smoking. Combine some salt and pepper on a small plate and dip each scallop in the mixture to coat both sides. Place the scallops, 4 at a time, in the oil and cook until brown, about 2 minutes on each side. Transfer to a piece of paper towel to drain. Coat more scallops in the salt and pepper and cook in the oil, until all the scallops are cooked.

5. WHEN the rice is tender but firm, in about 20 minutes, turn off the heat. Add the remaining ¼ cup broth and 2 tablespoons butter, and salt and pepper to taste, and stir well to combine with the rice.

6. To SERVE, spoon the risotto onto warmed dinner plates. Top each serving with 3 leaves of spinach and 3 scallops. Serve immediately.

Risotto with Shrimp, Periwinkles, and Peas

4 tablespoons unsalted butter

½ cup finely chopped onion

2 cups Arborio rice

½ cup dry white wine

6 cups chicken broth, preferably homemade (pages 27–28), heated

1 pound small raw shrimp, peeled and deveined

4 ounces fresh periwinkles, lightly steamed, shelled (see Box)

½ cup shelled fresh baby peas or defrosted frozen peas

Salt

Freshly ground black pepper

Makes 4 to 6 servings

This delicate, almost sweet-tasting risotto was served to me at the restaurant Cerasole in Cremona, Italy, where the risotto was prepared with canastrelli, a thumbnail-size shellfish that is not found in the United States. Periwinkles are a wonderful substitute, but you can omit them if they're not available.

1. HEAT 2 tablespoons of the butter in a heavy 4-quart pot over medium-high heat. Add the onion and cook, stirring, until the onion begins to soften, 2 to 3 minutes. Be careful not to brown it. Stir in the rice to coat the grains with the butter and onion mixture, and cook about 1 minute longer.

2. ADD the wine and stir until it is mostly absorbed by the rice. Add the broth, ½ cup at a time, stirring well after each addition. Wait until each addition of broth is almost completely absorbed before adding the next ½ cup. Reserve ¼ cup of broth to add at the end. After 15 minutes, add the shrimp, periwinkles, and peas.

3. WHEN the rice is tender but firm, about 5 minutes longer, turn off the heat. Add the remaining ¼ cup broth and 2 tablespoons butter, and salt and pepper to taste, and stir well to combine with the rice. Serve immediately.

PERIWINKLE PRIMER

Periwinkles are small mollusks with a spiral shell. They are commonly found clinging to rocks in shallow tidal marine areas. A specialty in Europe, especially in France where they are eaten raw from the shell, they are widespread along the northeastern coast of the United States and are available to buy in larger or ethnic fish markets. Periwinkles can be pulled from their shells raw with a long pin or needle (in Europe they stick a small cork into one end of a needle to make using it more functional). It's easier to lightly steam, or boil, the periwinkles until the lid of the shell, the *operculum*, opens. You may still have to use a pin, but the periwinkle inside comes out easily.

Risotto with Mussels and Tomatoes

FOR THE MUSSELS:

2 pounds fresh mussels in the shell, debearded and rinsed clean just before cooking, discarding any cracked or broken shells

¼ cup finely chopped shallots

1 cup dry white wine

FOR THE RISOTTO:

2 tablespoons olive oil

½ cup finely chopped shallots

2 large cloves garlic, peeled and pressed or finely chopped

1 cup chopped canned tomatoes, with their juice

2 cups Arborio rice

4 cups chicken broth, preferably homemade (pages 27–28), heated

¼ cup chopped fresh parsley leaves

1 tablespoon lemon juice

Salt

Freshly ground black pepper

Makes 4 to 6 servings

Farm-raised mussels are just about the only mussels available in fish markets these days. While some cooks dismiss farm-raised fish and seafood, I have come to particularly like the mussels—they're usually small, intensely sweet, and incredibly clean so they don't require much in the way of preparation. This risotto has tremendous flavor and plenty of mussels.

1. PREPARE the mussels: Combine the mussels in a large stockpot with the shallots and wine and place over high heat. When the liquid boils, cover and cook until most of the mussels open, about 5 minutes. Turn off the heat and leave covered 2 minutes. Strain the mussels, reserving the liquid (you should have about 2 cups). Set aside 18 mussels in their shells as a garnish, cover to keep warm. Remove the remaining mussels from the shells and coarsely chop. Set aside. Discard the shells.

2. PREPARE the risotto: Heat the oil in a heavy 4-quart pot over medium-high heat. Add the shallots and garlic and cook, stirring, until they begin to soften, 1 to 2 minutes. Add the rice and stir to coat the grains with the oil and onion mixture, and cook about 1 minute longer.

3. ADD the tomatoes, reserved mussel and wine liquid, and cook until it is mostly absorbed by the rice. Add the broth, ½ cup at a time, stirring well after each addition. Wait until each addition is almost completely absorbed before adding the next ½ cup. Reserve ¼ cup of broth to add at the end.

4. WHEN the rice is tender but firm, in about 20 minutes, turn off the heat. Add the remaining ¼ cup broth, the mussels, parsley, lemon juice, and salt and pepper to taste, and stir well to combine with the rice.

5. SERVE in warmed bowls with the reserved mussels as a garnish. Serve immediately.

Risotto with Oysters and Lemongrass Broth

3 stalks lemongrass (bottom 3 inches only), peeled, 2 stalks cut into 2-inch pieces and 1 stalk finely chopped

6 cups fish broth, preferably homemade (page 32), heated

2 tablespoons canola, corn, or other vegetable oil

½ cup finely chopped red onion

2 large cloves garlic, peeled and pressed or finely chopped

2 cups American short-grain rice (page 4)

½ cup rice wine (sake)

8 ounces shucked oysters, chopped, with their juice

½ cup shredded fresh basil leaves

Juice of ½ lemon

Salt

Freshly ground black pepper

1 tablespoon hot chili-flavored sesame oil (optional) (see Note)

Makes 4 to 6 servings

Note:
Hot chili-flavored sesame oil is available in Asian markets.

This risotto has an exotic but enticing flavor. You can substitute clams for the oysters. Be sure to peel the lemongrass before using it.

1. COMBINE the 2 cut stalks of lemongrass with the broth in a small saucepan over medium heat. Bring to a boil and simmer 10 minutes. Use a slotted spoon to remove the lemongrass, and discard.

2. HEAT the vegetable oil in a heavy 4-quart pot over medium-high heat. Add the onion, garlic, and finely chopped lemongrass and cook, stirring, until the onion begins to soften, 2 to 3 minutes. Be careful not to brown it. Stir in the rice to coat the grains with the oil and onion and lemongrass mixture, and cook about 1 minute longer.

3. ADD the wine and stir until it is mostly absorbed by the rice. Add the broth, ½ cup at a time, stirring well after each addition. Wait until each addition is almost completely absorbed before adding the next ½ cup. Reserve ¼ cup of broth to add at the end

4. WHEN the rice is tender but firm, in about 20 minutes, turn off the heat. Stir in the oysters with their juice, the basil, lemon juice, salt and pepper to taste, and chili oil if you are using it. Stir well to combine with the rice. Serve immediately.

Risotto with Lobster and Sea Vegetable

There is a wide variety of sea vegetables, a.k.a. seaweed, that you can choose from these days, but the distinctive thin black hijiki branches are my favorite to eat cooked. They add a subtle briny flavor to any dish. This Asian-flavored risotto is simple but luxurious.

1. HEAT the vegetable oil in a heavy 4-quart pot over medium-high heat. Add the ginger and stir to combine. Stir in the rice to coat the grains with the oil and ginger mixture, and cook about 1 minute longer.

2. ADD the rice wine and stir until it is mostly absorbed by the rice. Add the broth, ½ cup at a time, stirring well after each addition. Wait until each addition of broth is almost completely absorbed before adding the next ½ cup. Reserve ¼ cup of broth to add at the end.

3. WHEN the rice is tender but firm, in about 20 minutes, turn off the heat. Add the remaining broth, the carrot, hijiki, lobster, scallion, soy sauce, vinegar, and sesame oil, and salt and pepper to taste, and stir well to combine with the rice. Serve immediately, garnished with the sesame seeds.

Note:
You can find hijiki seaweed at most Asian markets, health food markets, and at all Whole Foods Markets nationwide.

2 tablespoons canola, corn, or other vegetable oil

1 tablespoon finely chopped, peeled fresh ginger root

2 cups American short-grain (page 4) or Arborio rice

¼ cup rice wine (sake)

6 cups fish broth, preferably homemade (page 32), heated

1 cup finely grated carrot

½ cup dried hijiki (see Note), soaked in warm water for 15 minutes and drained

8 ounces cooked lobster meat, roughly chopped (about 2 cups)

1 cup chopped scallion greens

1 tablespoon soy sauce, or more to taste

2 teaspoons rice wine vinegar

1 teaspoon sesame oil

Salt

Freshly ground pepper

2 tablespoons black sesame seeds, for garnish

Makes 4 to 6 servings

RISOTTO WITH LITTLE CLAMS, GARLIC, AND PARSLEY

3 pounds littleneck clams in
their shells, washed

½ cup water

3 tablespoons olive oil

¾ cup chopped onion

2 large cloves garlic, peeled and
pressed or finely chopped

Pinch red pepper flakes

¼ cup chopped fresh parsley
leaves

2 cups Arborio rice

½ cup dry white wine

6 cups chicken broth,
preferably homemade
(page 27–28), heated

Salt

Freshly ground black pepper

Makes 4 to 6 servings

A garlicky, simple clam sauce, the kind you use for pasta, is wonderful stirred into a risotto. The most important part of preparing the clams is making sure you avoid adding the sand that always comes with them. You don't have to do any complicated cleansing treatments to the clams if you steam the clams in their shells first and rinse them in water afterward. You can also use prepared chopped clams.

1. PLACE the clams in a large saucepan with the water, cover, and place over medium-high heat. Cook until the clam shells are open, 5 to 10 minutes. Uncover and allow to stand until cool enough to handle. Remove the clams from the shells, rinse to remove any sand, and chop. You should have about 1 cup chopped clams. Discard the shells and cooking liquid.

2. HEAT 1 tablespoon of the oil in a medium-size skillet over medium heat. Add ¼ cup of the chopped onion, the garlic, and the red pepper flakes and cook, stirring, until the onion begins to soften, 2 to 3 minutes. Be careful not to brown it. Stir in the clams and the parsley and cook about 2 minutes longer. Turn off the heat and set aside.

3. HEAT the remaining 2 tablespoons of oil in a 4-quart heavy pot over medium-high heat. Add the remaining onion and cook until it begins to soften, 2 to 3 minutes. Be careful not to brown it. Stir in the rice to coat the grains with the oil and onion mixture, and cook about 1 minute longer.

4. ADD the wine and stir until it is mostly absorbed by the rice. Add the broth, ½ cup at a time, stirring well after each addition. Wait until each addition is almost completely absorbed before adding the next ½ cup. Reserve ¼ cup broth to add at the end.

5. WHEN the rice is tender but firm, in about 20 minutes, turn off the heat. Add the remaining ¼ cup broth, the clam mixture, and salt and pepper to taste, and stir well to combine with the rice. Serve immediately.

HOT WATER

If you run short of broth, you can always add hot or simmering water to the risotto.

Risotto with Swordfish, Anchovies, Tomatoes, and Peas

2 tablespoons olive oil

4 whole flat anchovy fillets, packed in oil

1 cup finely chopped onion

2 cloves garlic, peeled and pressed or finely chopped

2 cups Arborio rice

1 cup dry white wine

1 cup chopped canned tomatoes, with their juice

5 cups fish broth, preferably homemade (page 32), heated

8 ounces fresh swordfish steak, skinned, cut into 1-inch cubes

¼ cup chopped fresh parsley leaves, rinsed

1 cup shelled fresh peas or defrosted frozen peas

Salt

Freshly ground black pepper

Makes 4 to 6 servings

This risotto captures the best flavors of Sicily. Swordfish, spada, is the most popular fish on the largest southern Italian island, and when combined with rice and tomatoes it makes a luscious dish. If you like a fishier taste, you can add more anchovies. In Sicily peas are used in many dishes including risotti; they add fresh flavor and color.

1. Heat the oil in a heavy 4-quart pot over medium-high heat. Add the anchovy fillets and cook, stirring, to break them up, about 1 minute. Add the onion and garlic and cook, stirring, until the onion begins to soften, 2 to 3 minutes. Be careful not to brown them. Stir in the rice to coat the grains with onion and oil mixture, and cook about 1 minute longer.

2. Add the wine and stir until it is mostly absorbed by the rice. Add the tomatoes with their juice and cook, stirring, until the liquid is mostly absorbed by the rice. Add the broth, ½ cup at a time, stirring well after each addition. Wait until each addition is almost completely absorbed before adding the next ½ cup. Reserve ¼ cup of broth to add at the end. When the rice has been cooking 15 minutes, stir in the swordfish.

3. When the rice is tender but firm, about 5 minutes longer, turn off the heat. Add the remaining ¼ cup broth, the parsley, peas, and salt and pepper to taste, and stir well to combine with the rice. Serve immediately.

RISOTTO WITH SPINACH AND SALMON

I sampled this risotto in a trattoria near the famous ancient Greek temples in Agrigento in Sicily. Like most Sicilian food, the flavors were strong and intense. Use fish broth for more authentic "fishy" flavor; use chicken broth for a milder taste.

1. HEAT the oil and 1 tablespoon of the butter in a heavy 4-quart pot over medium-high heat. Add the onion and cook until the onion begins to soften, 2 to 3 minutes. Be careful not to brown it. Stir in the rice to coat the grains with the oil and onion mixture, and cook about 1 minute longer.

2. ADD the wine and stir until it is mostly absorbed by the rice. Add the broth, ½ cup at a time, stirring well after each addition. Wait until each addition is almost completely absorbed before adding the next ½ cup. Reserve ¼ cup of broth to add at the end.

3. WHEN the rice is tender but firm, in about 20 minutes, stir in the salmon and spinach, and cook about 1 minute longer. Turn off the heat. Add the remaining ¼ cup broth and 1 tablespoon butter, and salt and pepper to taste. Stir well to combine. Serve immediately.

1 tablespoon olive oil

2 tablespoons unsalted butter

½ cup finely chopped onion

2 cups Arborio rice

½ cup dry white wine

6 cups fish broth or chicken broth, preferably homemade (pages 27–28 and 32), heated

8 ounces salmon fillet, skinned, cut into ½-inch pieces

One 10-ounce package frozen chopped spinach, cooked according to package directions and puréed

Salt

Freshly ground black pepper

Makes 4 to 6 servings

FOR THE FISH SOUP:

1 pound fish fillets, preferably from white-fleshed fish such as cod, pollack, monkfish, tilefish, tilapia, or flounder, cut into 1-inch pieces

3 tablespoons olive oil

2 large cloves garlic, peeled and pressed or finely chopped

Pinch saffron threads

2 tablespoons boiling water

1 medium-size leek, white part only, cut in half lengthwise, rinsed well between the layers, and thinly sliced crosswise

1 large rib celery, trimmed and thinly sliced

1 medium-size onion, peeled, cut in half, and thinly sliced

1 cup finely sliced fennel bulb

¼ teaspoon fennel seed

1 cup chopped canned tomatoes, with their juice

2 cups fish broth, preferably homemade (page 32), heated

Salt

This risotto was adapted from a savory Mediterranean fish stew that I often prepare. Use the flavorful, garlicky fish broth to cook the rice; serve the fish and vegetables from the soup over the finished risotto. The presentation is beautiful and the dish is divine.

1. PREPARE the fish soup: Combine the fish with 1 tablespoon of the olive oil and half the garlic in a small mixing bowl. Mix the saffron with the boiling water and pour over the fish. Mix well and allow to stand at room temperature 30 minutes.

2. HEAT the remaining 2 tablespoons of olive oil in a medium-size saucepan over medium-high heat. Add the remaining garlic, the leek, celery, onion, fresh fennel, and fennel seed and cook, stirring, until the vegetables begin to soften, 3 to 5 minutes. Add the tomatoes and the broth, season with salt to taste, and bring the liquid to a boil. Reduce the heat to low, partially cover the pot, and cook 15 minutes. Add the fish and cook 5 to 10 minutes longer or until the fish flakes easily with a fork. Strain the fish and vegetables from the broth, cover to keep warm, and set aside. Reserve the broth (you should have 4 to 5 cups) and combine with the other broth to yield 6 cups.

3. PREPARE the risotto: Heat the olive oil in a large heavy 4-quart pot over medium-high heat. Add the onion and garlic and cook, stirring, until the onion begins to soften, 2 to 3 minutes. Be careful not to brown it. Stir in the rice to coat the grains with the oil and onion mixture, and cook about 1 minute longer.

4. ADD the wine and stir until it is mostly absorbed by the rice. Add the broth, ½ cup at a time, stirring well after each addition. Wait until it is almost completely absorbed before adding the next ½ cup. Reserve ¼ cup of broth to add at the end.

5. WHEN the rice is tender but firm, in about 20 minutes, turn off the heat. Add the remaining ¼ cup broth, the parsley, and salt and pepper to taste, and stir well to combine. Serve the risotto in warmed soup bowls with some of the fish and vegetables on top. Garnish with parsley. Serve immediately.

FOR THE RISOTTO:

2 tablespoons olive oil

½ cup finely chopped onion

1 clove garlic, peeled and pressed or finely chopped

1 ½ cups Arborio rice

½ cup dry white wine

Salt

Freshly ground black pepper

¼ cup chopped fresh parsley leaves, rinsed

Makes 4 to 6 servings

LEMON AND CHIVE RISOTTO WITH OVEN-ROASTED RED SNAPPER FILLET

FOR THE FISH:

2 pounds red snapper fillet, preferably 6 small fillets each weighing ¼ to ⅓ pound, skinned

Juice of 1 lemon

Salt

2 tablespoons unsalted butter

FOR THE RISOTTO:

4 tablespoons unsalted butter

1 lemon, zest grated and juiced

½ cup finely chopped onion

2 cups Arborio rice

½ cup dry white wine

6 cups chicken broth, preferably homemade (pages 27–28), heated

2 tablespoons chopped fresh chives

3 tablespoons lemon juice

¼ cup chopped fresh parsley leaves, rinsed

Salt

Freshly ground black pepper

Makes 4 to 6 servings

This very lemony risotto is the perfect complement to almost any fish but it's particularly good with red snapper. Whole small fillets make an attractive serving presentation, but if you can't get small fillets, use larger ones and cut them into serving-size pieces before cooking.

The red snapper is lightly cooked with lemon and salt and garnished with parsley—the way they do it in Liguria. If red snapper is not available, use any mild-tasting, white-fleshed fish as a substitute.

1. PREPARE the fish: Preheat the oven to 450 degrees.

2. THIRTY minutes before you plan to cook the fish, place the snapper fillets on a glass or ceramic platter, squeeze the lemon juice over them, and season with salt to taste. Allow to stand at room temperature. To cook, melt the butter in a large ovenproof skillet over medium-high heat. Add the fillets skin side up and cook 1 minute; place the skillet in the oven. Cook until the fish flakes with a fork, 10 to 15 minutes. Remove from the oven and keep warm until ready to serve.

3. WHILE the fish is cooking, prepare the risotto: Heat 2 tablespoons of the butter in a heavy 4-quart pot over medium-high heat. Add the lemon zest and onion and cook, stirring, until the onion begins to soften, 2 to 3 minutes. Be careful not to brown it. Stir in the rice to coat the grains with the butter and onion mixture, and cook about 1 minute longer.

4. ADD the wine and stir until it is mostly absorbed by the rice. Add the broth, ½ cup at a time, stirring well after each addition. Wait until each addition is almost completely absorbed before adding the next ½ cup. Reserve ¼ cup of broth to add at the end.

5. WHEN the rice is tender but firm, in about 20 minutes, turn off the heat. Add the remaining ¼ cup broth and 2 tablespoons butter, the chives, lemon juice, 2 tablespoons of the parsley, and salt and pepper to taste.

6. TO SERVE, spoon the risotto onto warmed dinner plates. Top each serving with a piece of snapper and a sprinkling of parsley. Serve immediately.

1 cup cold water

½ cup dry white wine

1 lemon wedge (about ¼ lemon)

½ medium-size onion, peeled and halved

8 ounces skinned catfish fillets

1 tablespoon unsalted butter

1 tablespoon olive oil

3 tablespoons chopped onion

1 large clove garlic, peeled and finely chopped

½ teaspoon anchovy paste

2 tablespoons chopped fresh parsley leaves

2 cups Arborio rice

6 cups chicken broth, preferably homemade (pages 27–28), heated

Makes 4 to 6 servings

Catfish, pesce gatto, *is native to the rivers of Lombardy where this risotto has traditionally been prepared for as long as anyone has been keeping records.*

I sampled two variations on this dish. My favorite was the classic preparation made by Nadia Santini at her exquisite restaurant Dal Pescatore in Cannetto sull'Oglio near Mantova. She uses whole catfish, which are not readily available here. However, farmed catfish fillets are available, and they work very well in the classic recipe.

1. COMBINE the water, wine, lemon, and onion in a nonreactive large skillet or fish poacher and bring to a boil over medium-high heat. Reduce the heat to low, cover, and cook for 5 minutes. Add the catfish fillets, cover, and cook until the fish flakes easily with a fork, about 10 minutes. Uncover and allow to cool. Transfer the fish to a bowl and using a fork, gently break the fish into small flakes. You should have about 1 cup. Set aside.

2. HEAT the butter and olive oil in a heavy 4-quart pot over medium-high heat. Add the onion, garlic, anchovy paste; and parsley and cook, stirring, until the onion begins to soften, 2 to 3 minutes. Stir in the rice to coat the grains with the oil and onion mixture, and cook about 1 minute longer.

3. ADD the broth, ½ cup at a time, stirring well after each addition. Wait until each addition of broth is almost completely absorbed by the rice before adding the next ½ cup. Reserve ¼ cup of broth to add at the end.

4. WHEN the rice is tender but firm, in about 20 minutes, turn off the heat. Add the catfish, the remaining ¼ cup broth, and salt and pepper to taste, and stir well to combine with the rice. Serve immediately.

SPICY RISOTTO AI FRUTTI DI MARE

6 cups fish broth, preferably homemade (page 32), heated

¼ teaspoon red pepper flakes

3 tablespoons unsalted butter

1 tablespoon olive oil

½ cup finely chopped shallots

3 tablespoons finely chopped carrot

3 tablespoons finely chopped celery

1 ½ cups Arborio rice

½ cup dry white wine

8 ounces small squid, cleaned and thinly sliced, keeping the tentacles intact

8 medium-size raw shrimp, peeled (shells reserved), deveined, and finely chopped

4 ounces cooked lobster meat, shredded, or crab meat

¼ cup chopped fresh parsley leaves, rinsed

Salt

Freshly ground black pepper

Makes 4 to 6 servings

On the Tuscan coast of Italy, the fish broth is made with a hefty pinch of hot red pepper flakes which gives the risotto a definite kick, unlike the milder versions you find elsewhere in northern Italy.

This risotto calls for squid, shrimp, and lobster which are readily available in most good fish markets. You can add scallops or other seafood but if you do make substitutions in the recipe, try to keep the quantities and weights the same. You want to keep the rice and seafood in balance.

1. COMBINE the broth and the red pepper flakes in a medium-size saucepan over medium heat and bring to a boil. Lower the heat and simmer 10 minutes.

2. HEAT 1 tablespoon of the butter with the oil in a heavy 4-quart pot over medium-high heat. Add the shallots and cook, stirring, until the shallots begin to gradually soften, 1 to 2 minutes. Be careful not to brown them. Stir in the rice to coat the grains with the shallot and fat mixture, and cook about 1 minute longer.

3. ADD the wine and stir until it is mostly absorbed by the rice. Add the broth, ½ cup at a time, stirring well after each addition. Wait until each addition is almost completely absorbed before adding the next ½ cup. Reserve ¼ cup of broth to add at the end. After 15 minutes add the squid and shrimp.

4. WHEN the rice is tender but firm, about 5 minutes longer, turn off the heat. Add the remaining ¼ cup broth and 2 tablespoons butter, the lobster meat, parsley, and salt and pepper to taste, and stir well to combine with the rice. Serve immediately.

chapter SIX

Meat
risotti

*R*ustic or elegant, meat risotti—made with chicken, sausage, beef, rabbit, pork, quail, and even venison—are satisfying and filling enough to be served as a main course.

Traditional meat risotti in Italy are served in one of two ways: either with the meat stirred into the risotto, or with a *ragù* (meat sauce) or *spezzatino* (stew) served over the risotto. A contemporary way to serve meat risotti is with roasted or grilled meats set on top of the rice, making the risotto more of an accompaniment to the meat.

Most of these recipes call for small quantities of meat. When meat is combined with risotto, you will be surprised to find that even a small portion provides a substantial dinner. A pound of chicken breasts in risotto can serve four people. I recommend buying from a reliable, quality butcher, especially for some of the specialty meats. When you spend a little more, you will be able to taste the difference.

In the recipes where the risotto is prepared separately from the meat, you should feel free to also prepare and serve the risotto on its own without the meat. Most of these can be vegetarian risotti, when prepared with a vegetable broth, and make wonderful meatless first course or light entrée dishes.

The meat risotti in this book call for either meat or chicken broth; you can also use a vegetable broth (see pages 27–33).

RISOTTO OF BITTER GREENS AND PROSCIUTTO

This risotto has a marvelous flavor with an edge that's just sharp enough to nicely offset the richness of the prosciutto. Be sure to boil the broccoli rabe before adding it to the risotto; it helps to moderate the bitter taste. You can substitute watercress, arugula, or chicory for the escarole.

1. BRING a small saucepan of water to boil over high heat. Add the broccoli rabe and boil for 7 minutes. Drain. Rinse under cold water to stop the cooking and drain again. Coarsely chop to yield about 2 cups.

2. COMBINE 1 tablespoon of the butter and the oil in a heavy 4-quart pot over medium-high heat. Add the shallots and garlic and cook, stirring, until the shallots begin to soften, 1 to 2 minutes. Be careful not to brown them. Stir in the rice to coat the grains with the fat and shallot mixture, and cook about 1 minute longer.

3. ADD the wine and stir until it is mostly absorbed by the rice. Add the broth, ½ cup at time, stirring well after each addition. Wait until each addition of broth is almost completely absorbed before adding the next ½ cup, stirring frequently to prevent sticking. Reserve ¼ cup to add at the end. After 15 minutes add the escarole and the prosciutto.

4. WHEN the rice is tender but firm, about 5 minutes longer, turn off the heat; add the remaining ¼ cup broth and 1 tablespoon butter, the cooked broccoli rabe, cheese, and salt and pepper to taste. Stir well to combine with the rice. Serve immediately.

½ bunch broccoli rabe, thickest stems trimmed and discarded

2 tablespoons unsalted butter

1 tablespoon olive oil

½ cup finely chopped shallots

2 cloves garlic, peeled and pressed or finely chopped

2 cups Arborio rice

½ cup dry white wine

6 cups chicken or meat broth, preferably homemade (pages 27–29), heated

2 cups finely chopped escarole leaves (about 1 average head)

4 ounces prosciutto (cut into 2 or 3 thick slices), diced

½ cup freshly grated Italian parmesan cheese

Salt

Freshly ground black pepper

Makes 4 to 6 servings

SAFFRON RISOTTO WITH LAMB OSSO BUCCO

FOR THE LAMB:

3 tablespoons olive oil

1 medium-size onion, peeled and finely chopped

1 medium-size carrot, peeled and finely chopped

1 large rib celery, trimmed and finely chopped

2 large cloves garlic, peeled and finely chopped

3 small lamb shanks (each weighing about 1 pound), cut into 2-inch pieces

Salt

Freshly ground black pepper

⅓ cup dry white wine

1 cup chopped canned tomatoes, with their juice

3 cups chicken or meat broth, preferably homemade (pages 27–29), heated

FOR THE RISOTTO:

2 tablespoons unsalted butter

1 tablespoon olive oil

⅓ cup finely chopped shallots

2 cups Arborio rice

½ cup dry white wine

1 pinch saffron threads (see Box), pulverized

This recipe is a twist on the classic veal dish, and it makes a superb change. Use lamb shanks that are on the smaller side as larger shanks from older lambs tend to have a stronger, not always appealing, flavor. Have the butcher cut the shanks into pieces as the heavy bone is more than ordinary kitchen knives can handle.

1. PREPARE the lamb: Heat 2 tablespoons of the oil over medium heat in a heavy 6-quart flameproof casserole with a tight-fitting lid. Add the chopped vegetables and cook, uncovered, slowly until they begin to soften, about 5 minutes. Turn off the heat.

2. PREHEAT the oven to 350 degrees.

3. IN a 10-inch skillet, heat the remaining tablespoon of olive oil over medium-high heat and add the lamb shank pieces. Season the lamb with salt and pepper, and cook, turning the pieces, until they are well-browned all over, about 5 minutes. Transfer the lamb shanks to the casserole and arrange them in a single layer on top of the vegetables. Pour the wine into the skillet and cook over medium-high heat, scraping the browned bits on the bottom of the pan, until the wine is reduced by about half.

4. POUR the wine over the lamb shanks. Add the tomatoes and the broth to the casserole. Turn the heat under the casserole to high and bring the liquid to a boil. Turn off the heat. Cover the casserole and place in the preheated oven on the middle shelf. Allow to cook in the oven until the liquid has thickened and the meat is falling-off-the-bone tender, about 3 hours. Uncover and cook until the lamb shanks are beginning to brown, about ½ hour longer. Remove the casserole from the oven, cover, and

allow the lamb shanks to stand until ready to serve. (If the shanks have cooled, reheat over low stove heat when ready to serve.)

5. PREPARE the risotto: Combine 1 tablespoon of the butter and the olive oil in a heavy 4-quart pot over medium-high heat. Add the shallots and cook, stirring, until the shallots begin to soften, 1 to 2 minutes. Be careful not to brown them. Stir in the rice to coat the grains with the fat and shallot mixture, and cook about 1 minute longer.

6. ADD the wine and stir until it is mostly absorbed by the rice. Add the saffron and begin to add the broth, ½ cup at a time, stirring well after each addition. Wait until each addition of broth is almost completely absorbed before adding the next ½ cup. Reserve ¼ cup to add at the end.

7. WHEN the rice is tender but firm, in about 20 minutes, turn off the heat. Add the remaining ¼ cup broth and 1 tablespoon butter, the cheese, and salt and pepper to taste, and stir well to combine with the rice.

8. TO SERVE, spoon the risotto onto warmed dinner plates and place 2 or 3 pieces of lamb on top with some of the sauce from the meat. Garnish with a sprinkling of parsley. Serve immediately.

6 cups chicken or meat broth, preferably homemade (pages 27–29), heated

½ cup freshly grated Italian parmesan cheese

Salt

Freshly ground black pepper

2 tablespoons chopped fresh parsley leaves, rinsed

Makes 4 to 6 servings

SAFFRON SAVVY

Saffron is a luxury item and expensive. Buy pure saffron threads, not powdered saffron; that way you can be sure that what you get is unadulterated.

If needed, pulverize saffron threads in a mortar with a pestle or in a bowl with the back of a wooden spoon. One pinch of saffron threads yields about ⅛ teaspoon pulverized.

Red Cabbage Risotto with Roasted Pork Tenderloin and Caramelized Onions

FOR THE ONIONS:

1 tablespoon olive oil

2 large Vidalia or Spanish
    onions (1 to 2 pounds),
    peeled and thinly sliced

Salt

FOR THE ROAST PORK:

Two 1-pound pork tenderloins

Salt

Freshly ground black pepper

1 teaspoon olive oil

FOR THE RISOTTO:

2 tablespoons unsalted butter

1 tablespoon olive oil

½ cup finely chopped onion

2 cups Arborio rice

½ cup dry white wine

2 cups shredded red cabbage
    (about 6 ounces)

6 cups chicken or meat broth,
    preferably homemade (pages
    27–29), heated

½ cup freshly grated Italian
    parmesan cheese

Salt

*This risotto makes a dramatic presentation, but some assembly is
required: The red cabbage risotto is a bed on which the slices of pork
tenderloin rest; the pork is topped with a mound of golden brown
onions and a sprinkling of parsley. The whole dish can be completed, start to finish, in 30 minutes. The onions require the most
cooking, a half hour, and the risotto and pork take only 20 minutes.
Serve with a green salad for a perfect meal.*

1. PREPARE the onions: Heat the oil in a large 10-inch skillet over medium heat. Add the onions and season with
   salt to taste. Reduce the heat to low, and cook, stirring
   occasionally, until the onions turn a golden caramel
   color, about 30 minutes. (These can be prepared hours
   in advance and reheated just before serving.)

2. PREHEAT the oven to 450 degrees.

3. PREPARE the roast pork: Season the pork with salt and
   pepper. Heat the teaspoon of oil over high heat in a
   flameproof roasting pan, preferably enameled cast iron,
   or ovenproof skillet large enough to hold the tenderloins. When the oil is smoking, add the tenderloins and
   brown all sides, about 4 minutes.

4. IMMEDIATELY place the roasting pan in the oven on the
   middle shelf and roast until the meat turns a creamy
   white color and is cooked through but not dry, about
   20 minutes. Remove the roasting pan from the oven and
   cover loosely with a piece of aluminum foil to keep the
   pork warm until ready to serve.

5. WHILE the pork is roasting, prepare the risotto: Heat 1 tablespoon of the butter with the olive oil in a heavy 4-quart pot over medium-high heat. Add the onion and cook, stirring, until the onion begins to soften, 2 to 3 minutes. Be careful not to brown it. Stir in the rice to coat the grains with the fat and onion mixture, and cook about 1 minute longer.

6. ADD the wine and stir until it is mostly absorbed by the rice. Add the cabbage and begin to add the broth, ½ cup at a time, stirring well after each addition. Wait until each addition of broth is almost completely absorbed before adding the next ½ cup. Reserve ¼ cup of the broth to add at the end.

7. WHEN the rice is tender but firm, in about 20 minutes, turn off the heat. Add the remaining ¼ cup broth and 1 tablespoon butter, the cheese, and salt and pepper to taste, and stir well to combine with the rice.

8. TO SERVE, slice each pork loin into 1-inch thick pieces. Spoon the risotto onto warmed dinner plates. Top each serving with 3 slices of meat and arrange a mound of the onions on top. Sprinkle each dish with a teaspoon of parsley. Serve immediately.

Freshly ground black pepper

2 tablespoons chopped fresh parsley leaves, rinsed

Makes 4 to 6 servings

TASTE TEST

Taste the risotto frequently toward the end of the cooking process as the total amount of cooking time may vary by 2 to 3 minutes.

MERLOT RISOTTO WITH TENDERLOIN OF BEEF

FOR THE MEAT:

One 2-pound center cut beef tenderloin

1 tablespoon olive oil

Salt

Freshly ground black pepper

FOR THE RISOTTO:

2 tablespoons unsalted butter

2 tablespoons olive oil

½ cup finely chopped shallots

2 cups Arborio rice

2 cups merlot or other dry red wine, at room temperature

4 ½ cups chicken or meat broth, preferably homemade (pages 27–29), heated

½ cup freshly grated Italian parmesan cheese

2 tablespoons chopped fresh parsley leaves, rinsed

Salt

Freshly ground black pepper

Makes 4 to 6 servings

One of the most classic of all Italian risotti is risotto al barolo made with Italy's premier red wine, Barolo, from the northwestern region of Piedmont. A California Merlot is more affordable these days and turns out a comparable risotto; the wine turns the rice a deep mahogany color and gives it a marvelously rich flavor. This simple but savory risotto is the perfect accompaniment to roasted beef tenderloin.

1. PREHEAT the oven to 450 degrees.

2. PREPARE the meat: Trim any excess fat from the beef and generously season with salt and pepper. Heat the oil in a flameproof roasting pan, large enough to hold the meat, preferably made of enameled cast iron, or in an oven-proof skillet over medium-high heat. When the oil is smoking, add the meat and brown on all sides, about 4 to 5 minutes total.

3. PLACE the roasting pan or skillet in the oven on the top shelf and roast for 18 minutes exactly. The meat will be medium rare. Remove from the oven, and cover loosely with aluminum foil to keep warm until ready to serve.

4. WHILE the meat is roasting, prepare the risotto: Heat 1 tablespoon of the butter with the olive oil in a heavy 4-quart pot over medium-high heat. Add the shallots and cook, stirring, until they begin to soften, 1 to 2 minutes. Be careful not to brown them. Stir in the rice to coat the grains with the fat and shallot mixture, and cook about 1 minute longer.

5. ADD the wine, ½ cup at a time, stirring well after each addition. When all the wine has been added, begin to add the broth, ½ cup at a time, stirring well after each addition. Wait until each addition of broth is almost completely absorbed before adding the next ½ cup. Reserve ¼ cup of the broth to add at the end.

6. WHEN the rice is tender but firm, in about 20 minutes, turn off the heat. Add the remaining ¼ cup broth and 1 tablespoon butter, the cheese, parsley, and salt and pepper to taste, and stir well to combine with the rice.

7. TO SERVE, slice the tenderloin into 1-inch-thick slices. Spoon the risotto onto warmed dinner plates. Top with 2 or 3 slices of beef tenderloin. Serve immediately.

RISOTTO WITH CHORIZO, CHIPOTLES, AND BLACK BEANS

2 tablespoons olive oil

1 medium-size onion, peeled and thinly sliced

2 cloves garlic, peeled and pressed or finely chopped

½ cup chopped green bell pepper

2 dry chipotle chilies combined with ½ cup boiling water for 10 minutes (or use canned), drained, seeded, and chopped

Pinch ground cardamom

2 cups American short-grain rice (page 4) or Arborio rice

½ cup dry white wine

8 ounces chorizo sausage (1 link), cut into ½-inch dice

6 cups chicken or meat broth, preferably homemade (pages 27–29), heated

¼ cup chopped fresh cilantro leaves

½ cup cooked black beans, rinsed and drained if canned

1 tablespoon lime juice

Salt

Freshly ground black pepper

Makes 4 to 6 servings

This is a smoky, spicy dish that is both hearty and heartwarming with its strong flavors and rustic texture.

Dry and canned chipotles are available in Latin American food stores and some well-stocked supermarkets. If using canned chipotles, after opening transfer chipotles to an airtight container and refrigerate for up to 3 months.

1. HEAT the oil in a heavy 4-quart pot over medium-high heat. Add the onion, garlic, and green pepper and cook, stirring, until the vegetables begin to soften, 2 to 3 minutes. Be careful not to brown them. Add the chipotles and cardamom and stir to combine. Stir in the rice to coat the grains with the oil and vegetable mixture, and cook about 1 minute longer.

2. ADD the wine and stir until it is mostly absorbed by the rice. Add the chorizo sausage and gradually add the broth, ½ cup at a time, stirring well after each addition. Wait until each addition of broth is almost completely absorbed by the rice before adding the next ½ cup. Reserve ¼ cup of the broth to add at the end.

3. WHEN the rice is tender but firm, in about 20 minutes, turn off the heat. Add the remaining ¼ cup broth, the cilantro, black beans, lime juice, and salt and pepper to taste, and stir well to combine with the rice. Serve immediately.

COUNTRY-STYLE RISOTTO WITH BUTTERNUT SQUASH AND SPICY SAUSAGE

This rustic and hearty risotto is a great main course to serve in the winter with a green salad and some warm crusty bread.

1. In a small skillet cook the sausage over medium heat until it is browned and fully cooked, about 10 minutes. Turn off the heat and set aside.

2. Heat the olive oil in a heavy 4-quart pot over medium-high heat. Add the onion, garlic, carrot, and celery and cook, stirring, until the vegetables begin to soften, 2 to 3 minutes. Be careful not to brown them. Stir in the rice to coat the grains with the oil and vegetable mixture, and cook about 1 minute longer.

3. Add the fennel seed, thyme, and wine and stir until it is mostly absorbed by the rice. Add the butternut squash and stir to combine. Gradually add the broth, ½ cup at a time, stirring well after each addition. Wait until each addition of broth is almost completely absorbed by the rice before adding the next ½ cup. Reserve ¼ cup of the broth to add at the end.

4. When the rice is tender but firm, in about 20 minutes, turn off the heat. Add the remaining ¼ cup broth, the sausage, spinach, cheese, and salt and pepper to taste, and stir to combine with the rice. Serve immediately.

8 ounces spicy fresh sausage such as chorizo or Italian sausage, cut into ½-inch pieces

2 tablespoons olive oil

½ cup finely chopped onion

2 large cloves garlic, peeled and pressed or finely chopped

¼ cup finely chopped carrot

¼ cup finely chopped celery

2 cups Arborio rice

¼ teaspoon fennel seed

2 tablespoons fresh thyme leaves or 2 teaspoons dried

½ cup dry white wine

4 ounces peeled butternut squash, grated (to yield 1 cup)

6 cups chicken or meat broth, preferably homemade (pages 27–29), heated

2 cups packed, washed, fresh spinach leaves, rinsed, stemmed, dried, and roughly chopped

½ cup freshly grated Italian parmesan cheese

Salt

Freshly ground black pepper

Makes 4 to 6 servings

Sun-Dried Tomato *Ragù* and Fennel Risotto

FOR THE *RAGÙ*:

2 tablespoons olive oil

1 medium-size onion, peeled and finely chopped

1 small carrot, peeled and finely chopped

4 ounces fennel bulb (about ½ small bulb), stalks removed and discarded, bulb finely chopped

1 pound ground meat (lean beef, veal, pork, turkey, or a combination)

Salt

Freshly ground black pepper

¼ teaspoon fennel seed

½ cup dry white wine

3 cups chopped canned tomatoes, with their juice

¼ cup chopped fresh parsley leaves, rinsed

½ cup chopped sun-dried tomatoes packed in oil

FOR THE RISOTTO:

2 tablespoons olive oil

⅓ cup finely chopped onion

The fennel and sun-dried tomatoes give a boost of flavor to a conventional ragù that complements a fennel risotto.

1. PREPARE the *ragù:* Heat the oil in a heavy 4-quart saucepan over medium-high heat. Add the onion, carrot, and fresh fennel and cook, stirring, until the vegetables begin to soften, about 5 minutes. Add the meat, and cook, using a spoon to break the meat into small pieces, until the meat is thoroughly cooked and loses its raw color, about 5 minutes. Season with salt and pepper to taste, and add the fennel seed. Add the wine and cook until it has mostly evaporated, 3 to 5 minutes. Add the tomatoes, reduce the heat to medium low and cook the sauce until thickened, about 45 minutes. Stir in the parsley and the sun-dried tomatoes and set aside. Reheat before serving.

2. PREPARE the risotto: Heat the oil in a heavy 4-quart pot over medium-high heat. Add the onion and fennel and cook, stirring, until the vegetables begin to soften, 2 to 3 minutes. Be careful not to brown them. Stir in the rice until the grains are coated with the oil and vegetable mixture, and cook about 1 minute longer.

3. ADD the fennel seed and begin to add the broth, ½ cup at a time, stirring well after each addition. Wait until each addition of broth is almost completely absorbed before adding the next ½ cup. Reserve ¼ cup of the broth to add at the end.

4. WHEN the rice is tender but firm, in about 20 minutes, turn off the heat. Add the remaining ¼ cup broth, the cheese, and salt and pepper to taste, and stir well to combine with the rice.

5. TO SERVE, spoon the risotto onto warmed dinner plates. Top with some of the *ragù*. Garnish each serving with a sprinkling of parsley. Serve immediately.

4 ounces fennel bulb (about ½ small bulb), stalks removed and discarded, bulb cut in half lengthwise and thinly sliced crosswise

2 cups Arborio rice

⅛ teaspoon fennel seed

6 cups chicken or meat broth, preferably homemade (pages 27–29), heated

⅓ cup freshly grated Italian parmesan cheese

Salt

Freshly ground black pepper

¼ cup chopped fresh parsley leaves, rinsed

Makes 4 to 6 servings

1 tablespoon olive oil

3 pounds boneless lamb stew
meat, from the leg or the
shoulder, trimmed of fat and
cut into 1-inch pieces

Salt

Freshly ground black pepper

1 large leek, white part only, cut
in half lengthwise, rinsed
well between the layers, and
thinly sliced across (to yield
2 cups)

1 medium-size carrot, peeled
and finely chopped

1 large clove garlic, peeled and
pressed or finely chopped

½ cup dry white wine

½ cup chopped canned
tomatoes, with their juice

2 tablespoons tomato paste

6 sprigs fresh thyme; or
1 teaspoon dried

1 bay leaf

About 1 ½ cups meat broth,
preferably homemade (page
29), heated

Grated Grana Risotto (page 111)

Makes 4 to 6 servings

Savory and rustic, this spezzatino *has a marvelous flavor that
comes from the lamb and tomatoes as they cook slowly with herbs
and seasonings for a long time. Note that the lamb is cut into particularly small pieces because you want to end up with meat that
won't require any cutting.*

1. PREHEAT the oven to 350 degrees.

2. HEAT the oil in a heavy 4-quart flameproof casserole
   with a tight-fitting lid over medium heat. Add the meat,
   season with salt and pepper to taste, and cook, uncovered, stirring, until the pieces of meat are beginning to
   brown, about 5 minutes. Remove the meat from the pot,
   transfer to a bowl, and set aside.

3. ADD the leek, carrot, and garlic to the casserole and
   cook, stirring, until the leek begins to soften, 3 to 5 minutes. Add the wine, scraping the browned bits on the
   bottom of the pot, and cook until the liquid is reduced
   by half, 3 to 5 minutes.

4. RETURN the lamb to the casserole; stir in the tomatoes,
   tomato paste, thyme, and bay leaf. Add enough broth to
   cover. Cover the casserole, place on the middle shelf in
   the oven and bake until the meat is tender and the liquid
   has thickened, about 2 hours. Serve over Grated Grana
   Risotto.

Spezzatino of Veal with Prosciutto and Red Wine

The veal, prosciutto, and red wine cook into a deliciously rich and thick, luscious stew with an honest, hearty flavor.

1. PREHEAT the oven to 350 degrees.

2. HEAT 1 tablespoon of the oil in a heavy 4-quart flame-proof casserole with a tight-fitting lid over medium heat. Add the onion, garlic, and prosciutto and cook, stirring, until the onions are soft and beginning to turn translucent, 3 to 5 minutes. Remove the onion and prosciutto mixture from the casserole and set aside.

3. ADD the remaining 2 tablespoons of the oil to the casserole over medium heat. Dredge the meat in the flour, shaking off any excess; add the meat to the casserole, and season with salt and pepper to taste. Cook, stirring, for about 3 minutes until the pieces of meat are beginning to brown. Add the wine and cook, scraping the browned bits on the bottom of the casserole, until the wine is reduced by about half, 3 to 5 minutes.

4. ADD the onion mixture to the meat. Stir in the broth, tomatoes, thyme, parsley, and bay leaf. Cover the casserole and place on the middle shelf in the oven. Bake until the meat is fork-tender and the sauce has thickened, 1 ½ to 2 hours. Season with salt and pepper to taste. Serve over Grated Grana Risotto.

3 tablespoons olive oil

1 cup finely chopped onion

2 cloves garlic, peeled and pressed or finely chopped

6 ounces imported prosciutto, preferably cut in 2 or 3 thick slices, diced

3 pounds boneless veal shoulder, cut into 1-inch pieces

¼ cup unbleached white flour spread in a large dish

Salt

Freshly ground black pepper

1 ½ cups dry red wine such as Montepulciano

1 cup chicken or meat broth, preferably homemade (pages 27–29), heated

1 cup chopped canned tomatoes, with their juice

2 tablespoons chopped fresh thyme leaves, or 1 teaspoon dried

¼ cup chopped fresh parsley leaves, rinsed

1 bay leaf

Salt

Freshly ground black pepper

Grated Grana Risotto (page 111)

Makes 4 to 6 servings

1 pound boneless rabbit meat,
   cut from a 2- to 3-pound
   fresh rabbit, cut into 1-inch
   pieces

1 cup dry red wine, such as a
   Montepulciano

2 large cloves garlic, peeled and
   pressed or finely chopped

2 tablespoons olive oil

Salt

Freshly ground black pepper

1 tablespoon unbleached white
   flour

2 cups chicken or meat broth,
   preferably homemade
   (pages 27–29), heated

¼ teaspoon red pepper flakes

1 cup chopped canned tomatoes, with their juice

2 tablespoons tomato paste

1 sprig fresh thyme, or
   ½ teaspoon dried

2 tablespoons chopped fresh
   parsley leaves, rinsed

Grated Grana Risotto
   (page 111)

Makes 4 to 6 servings

This is a hearty and highly seasoned stew. Use only a fresh (not frozen) small rabbit from a quality meat market or butcher. This is a great year-round dish because it cooks on the stove and not in the oven.

1. COMBINE the rabbit meat, red wine, and garlic in a large glass or other nonreactive mixing bowl. Stir well to combine, cover, and refrigerate 3 to 5 hours or overnight. Drain and discard marinade.

2. HEAT the oil in a heavy 4-quart flameproof casserole over medium-high heat. Add the rabbit, season with salt and pepper to taste, and cook, stirring, until the meat begins to brown, about 5 minutes. Sprinkle the flour over the meat and stir until the flour begins to dissolve into the pan juices. Add ½ cup of the broth; use a wooden spoon to scrape the browned bits on the bottom of the casserole.

3. ADD the red pepper flakes, tomatoes, tomato paste, thyme, and the remaining broth. Bring the liquid to a boil, cover, and reduce the heat to low. Simmer, covered, until the meat is very tender, about 45 minutes. Season with salt to taste, stir in the parsley, and serve over Grated Grana Risotto.

GRATED GRANA RISOTTO

Plain and simple, this risotto has a great, rich taste that's perfectly suited to complement and accompany the flavorful stews, spezzatini. Serve this risotto with the meat and juices on top. In Italy the risotto is sometimes molded into a circular shape with the stew served inside the ring.

1. COMBINE the oil and 1 tablespoon of the butter in a heavy 4-quart pot over medium-high heat. When the butter melts, add the onion and cook, stirring, until the onion begins to soften, 2 to 3 minutes. Be careful not to brown it. Stir in the rice to coat the grains with the fat and onion mixture, and cook about 1 minute longer.

2. ADD the wine and stir until it is mostly absorbed by the rice. Add the broth, ½ cup at a time, stirring well after each addition. Wait until each addition of broth is almost completely absorbed by the rice before adding the next ½ cup. Reserve ¼ cup of the broth to add at the end.

3. WHEN the rice is tender but firm, in about 20 minutes, turn off the heat. Add the remaining ¼ cup broth and 1 tablespoon butter, and the cheese, and stir well to combine with the rice. Serve on warmed dinner plates topped with a *spezzatino.*

1 tablespoon olive oil

2 tablespoons unsalted butter

½ cup finely chopped onion

2 cups Arborio rice

½ cup dry white wine

6 cups chicken or meat broth, preferably homemade (pages 27–29), heated

¾ cup freshly grated grana cheese

Spezzatino of lamb, veal, or rabbit (pages 108–10)

Makes 4 to 6 servings

RISOTTO WITH CELERIAC, PANCETTA, AND ROASTED VENISON

FOR THE RISOTTO:

8 ounces celeriac (celery root), peeled and cut into 2-inch pieces

Salt

4 ounces pancetta, chopped

2 tablespoons unsalted butter

½ cup finely chopped onion

2 large ribs celery, trimmed and finely chopped

2 cups Arborio rice

½ cup dry white wine

6 cups chicken or meat broth, preferably homemade (pages 27–29), heated

½ cup freshly grated Italian parmesan cheese

2 tablespoons finely chopped fresh parsley leaves, rinsed

FOR THE VENISON:

Two 1-pound venison tenderloins

Salt

Freshly ground black pepper

1 tablespoon olive oil

Makes 4 to 6 servings

This risotto has a distinctive celery flavor—from the celeriac (celery root) as well as lots of celery—that complements the distinctive taste of the venison.

1. PREHEAT the oven to 450 degrees.

2. PREPARE the risotto: Combine the celeriac, water to cover, and salt to taste in a small saucepan over medium-high heat. When the water boils, reduce the heat to medium-low, cover the pan, and cook until the celeriac is tender when pierced with a sharp knife, 25 to 30 minutes. Transfer the celeriac with its liquid to the work bowl of a food processor or blender and purée. Set aside.

3. THE risotto: Place the pancetta in a heavy 4-quart pot over medium heat. Cook, stirring, until the pancetta has rendered all its fat and is brown, about 5 minutes. Use a slotted spoon to remove the pancetta from the pot; set aside. Pour off all but 1 tablespoon of fat from the pot and discard. Add 1 tablespoon of the butter to the pot with the fat and heat over medium-high heat. When the butter melts, add the onion and celery and cook, stirring, until the onion begins to soften, 2 to 3 minutes. Be careful not to brown it. Stir in the rice to coat the grains with the fat and onion mixture, and cook about 1 minute longer.

4. ADD the wine and stir until it is mostly absorbed by the rice. Add the broth, ½ cup at a time, stirring well after each addition. Wait until each addition of broth is almost completely absorbed before adding the next ½ cup. Reserve ¼ cup of the broth to add at the end.

5. WHILE the risotto is cooking, prepare the venison: Season the venison with salt and pepper. Heat the oil in a small flameproof roasting pan, preferably enameled cast iron and large enough to hold both tenderloins, over medium-high heat. When the oil is smoking, add the venison and brown on all sides, about 4 to 5 minutes total. Immediately place it in the oven on the top shelf and roast exactly 10 minutes. The meat will be rare. Remove the roasting pan from the oven and cover loosely with a piece of aluminum foil to keep the venison warm until ready to serve.

6. WHEN the rice is tender but firm, in about 20 minutes, turn off the heat. Add the remaining ¼ cup broth and 1 tablespoon butter, the puréed celeriac, cooked pancetta, cheese, parsley, and salt and pepper to taste, and stir well to combine with the rice.

7. TO SERVE, slice each tenderloin of venison crosswise into 6 pieces. Spoon the risotto onto warmed dinner plates and arrange slices of the venison on top of the risotto. Serve immediately.

RISOTTO WITH LENTILS, ARTICHOKES, AND ROASTED RABBIT

FOR THE RABBIT:

4 boned rabbit loins, cut from two whole 2-pound rabbits

Salt

Freshly ground black pepper

1 tablespoon olive oil

1 sprig fresh rosemary

FOR THE RISOTTO:

1 medium-size artichoke

2 tablespoons olive oil

Salt

½ cup water

2 tablespoons unsalted butter

⅓ cup finely chopped shallots

1 ½ cups Arborio rice

½ cup dry white wine

3 tablespoons brown lentils

5 ½ cups chicken or meat broth, preferably homemade (pages 27–29), heated

½ cup freshly grated Italian parmesan cheese

¼ cup chopped fresh parsley leaves, rinsed

Salt

Freshly ground black pepper

Makes 4 to 6 servings

This recipe was inspired by a risotto I enjoyed at the restaurant Valentino in Santa Monica, California. Owner Pierro Selvaggio prepares this risotto with the small, dark Italian lentils, lenticche di Castelluccio from Umbria, which you can buy in Italian specialty stores, but you can use any lentils to prepare this dish.

1. PREHEAT the oven to 400 degrees.

2. PREPARE the rabbit: Roll the rabbit loins and secure the ends with toothpicks or tie each loin with a small piece of string. Sprinkle with salt and pepper to taste. Heat the oil in a medium-size flameproof roasting pan, preferably enameled cast iron, over medium-high heat. When the oil is smoking, add the loins and brown on all sides, about 4 to 5 minutes total. Pull the leaves from the sprig of rosemary and sprinkle over the rabbit.

3. PLACE the roasting pan in the oven on the top shelf, reduce the heat to 350 degrees, and roast 30 minutes. Remove from the oven and cover loosely with a piece of aluminum foil to keep warm until ready to serve.

4. WHILE the rabbit is roasting, prepare the risotto: Cut the artichoke stem, leaving about 1 inch from the base. Pull off the tough, dark green leaves, starting with the leaves closest to the stem, until only the interior yellow-green leaves are visible. Do not use a scissors or knife for this; the leaves will break naturally at the point where the tough part ends and the tender part begins. Using a serrated knife, cut 2 inches off the top of the artichoke, peel the stem, and trim around the base of the artichoke. Cut the artichoke into quarters lengthwise. Cut out the

fuzzy choke from each quarter and the sharp leaves just above it. Thinly slice the artichoke quarters and chop to yield approximately 1 cup.

5. HEAT 1 tablespoon of the oil in a small saucepan over medium heat. Add the chopped artichoke, season with salt to taste, and cook, stirring, about 2 minutes. Add ½ cup of water to the pan, cover, reduce the heat to low, and cook until the water is evaporated and the artichoke is tender, about 20 minutes. Turn off the heat and set aside.

6. HEAT the remaining tablespoon of oil with 1 tablespoon of butter in a heavy 4-quart pot over medium-high heat. Add the shallots and cook, stirring, until they begin to soften, 1 to 2 minutes. Be careful not to brown them. Stir in the rice to coat the grains with the butter and shallot mixture, and cook about 1 minute longer.

7. ADD the wine and stir until it is mostly absorbed by the rice. Add the lentils and begin to add the broth, ½ cup at a time, stirring well after each addition. Wait until each addition of broth is almost completely absorbed before adding the next ½ cup. Reserve ¼ cup of the broth to add at the end.

8. WHEN the rice is tender but firm, in about 20 minutes, turn off the heat. Stir in the cooked artichokes, the remaining ¼ cup broth and 1 tablespoon butter, the cheese, parsley, and salt and pepper to taste, and stir well until combined with the rice.

9. TO SERVE, remove the toothpicks or string from the rabbit loins and slice each loin crosswise into 4 pieces. Spoon the risotto onto warmed dinner plates. Top each serving with pieces of the rabbit. Serve immediately.

Herb Risotto with Crispy Quail

FOR THE QUAIL:

12 semiboneless quail (see Note)

Juice of 2 lemons

2 large cloves garlic, peeled and pressed or finely chopped

2 tablespoons olive oil

Salt

Freshly ground black pepper

FOR THE RISOTTO:

3 tablespoons unsalted butter

1 tablespoon olive oil

½ cup finely chopped shallots

2 cups Arborio rice

½ cup dry white wine

6 cups chicken broth, preferably homemade (pages 27–28), heated

½ cup chopped fresh herb leaves including sage, tarragon, chives, basil, and parsley; or 3 tablespoons mixed dried herbs such as prepared *herbes de Provence*

⅓ cup freshly grated Italian parmesan cheese

Salt

Freshly ground black pepper

Makes 4 to 6 servings

Since semiboneless quail became available several years ago, cooking quail couldn't be easier. These quail are seasoned and marinated and cooked quickly—in 8 minutes under the broiler while you prepare the herb-infused risotto. The combination of the aromatic, flavorful risotto and crispy quail is simply delicious and the presentation is impressive.

1. PREPARE the quail: At least 1 ¼ hours before you plan to cook them, place the quail in a large glass or other nonreactive shallow baking pan, large enough to hold them in a single layer, and add the lemon juice, garlic, olive oil, and salt to taste. Do not remove the stainless-steel, V-shaped pins; they keep the quail flat during cooking. Turn the quail over a few times to coat them thoroughly with the marinade. Marinate, covered with plastic wrap, in the refrigerator for 1 to 3 hours. Allow to stand at room temperature for a maximum of 20 minutes before you plan to cook them.

2. PREHEAT the oven broiler.

3. PLACE the quail in a single layer in a large roasting pan or on a broiling rack. Season with pepper to taste. Place on the shelf closest to the broiler and cook until brown and crispy, exactly 4 minutes on each side. Remove the roasting pan from the oven and cover loosely with a piece of aluminum foil to keep the quail warm until ready to serve. Before serving, pull the stainless-steel pins from the quail.

4. PREPARE the risotto: Combine 2 tablespoons of the butter and the olive oil in a heavy 4-quart pot over medium-high heat. Add the shallots and cook, stirring,

until the shallots begin to soften, 1 to 2 minutes. Be careful not to brown them. Stir in the rice to coat the grains with the fat and shallot mixture, and cook about 1 minute longer.

5. ADD the wine and stir until it is mostly absorbed by the rice. Add the broth, ½ cup at a time, stirring well after each addition. Wait until each addition of broth is almost completely absorbed before adding the next ½ cup. Reserve ¼ cup of the broth to add at the end.

6. WHEN the rice is tender but firm, in about 20 minutes, turn off the heat. Add the remaining ¼ cup broth and 1 tablespoon butter, the herbs, cheese, and salt and pepper to taste, and stir well until the butter melts and the cheese is incorporated into the rice.

7. TO SERVE, spoon the risotto onto warmed dinner plates. Top each serving with 2 or 3 quail. Serve immediately.

Note:
Semiboneless quail are usually available through specialty butchers. Since the quail are perishable, many butchers freeze them as soon as they get them in their stores. Fresh, unfrozen quail are preferable if you can get them, but frozen quail can be perfectly good as well. Boneless quail come with a stainless-steel, V-shaped pin in the breast cavity which helps keep them flat during cooking. Leave the pins in until the quail are cooked and remove them just before serving.

TERRANCE BRENNAN'S DUCK RISOTTO

1 leg of duck confit (see Note)

**1 ounce dried porcini mush-
rooms (about ⅔ cup
depending on the size of the
porcini pieces)**

1 cup water, boiling

4 tablespoons unsalted butter

**4 ounces fresh shiitake or other
mushrooms, stemmed and
thinly sliced (to yield 2 cups)**

**½ cup grated peeled butternut
squash, uncooked**

**2 large cloves garlic, peeled and
pressed or finely chopped**

1 tablespoon olive oil

½ cup finely chopped onion

2 cups Arborio rice

½ cup dry white wine

**6 cups chicken or meat broth,
preferably homemade (pages
27–29), heated**

**½ cup freshly grated Italian
parmesan cheese**

**1 tablespoon chopped fresh
sage leaves**

**¼ cup chopped fresh parsley
leaves, rinsed**

Salt

Freshly ground black pepper

*Terrance Brennan is the chef and owner of the New York City
restaurant Picholine. He has cooked in some of the best kitchens in
Italy and New York and has real reverence for risotto, never precooking it for convenience. His complex duck risotto has a wonderful combination of rustic flavors. This recipe is adapted from his
instructions.*

1. PREHEAT the oven to 275 degrees.

2. PUT the duck leg on a foil-covered baking sheet, place in
   the oven, and warm through until the skin comes off
   easily, about 10 minutes. Remove the duck skin and use
   your fingers to pull the duck meat from the bones; chop
   the duck meat into small, 1-inch pieces and set aside.
   (Optional: Place the duck skin on a baking sheet and
   broil until crisp, drain on paper towel, and slice for a garnish on the finished risotto.)

3. COMBINE the porcini with the boiling water in a heat-
   proof 2-cup glass measuring cup. Allow to stand at least
   15 minutes. Drain the porcini, rinse them, and chop
   coarsely. Strain the soaking liquid and add it to the
   broth. Set aside.

4. HEAT 1 tablespoon of the butter in a small saucepan over
   medium heat. When the butter melts, add the fresh
   mushrooms, season with salt to taste, and cook, stirring,
   until the mushrooms are tender, about 5 minutes. Remove the mushrooms from the pan and set aside. Melt
   another tablespoon of butter in the pan, add the butternut squash, and cook, stirring, until tender, 2 to 3 minutes. Add the cooked mushrooms, the soaked porcini,
   the duck, and half the garlic to the pan. Cook, stirring,
   until the ingredients are combined, about 1 minute.
   Set aside.

5. COMBINE 1 tablespoon of butter and the olive oil in a heavy 4-quart pot over medium-high heat. Add the onion and remaining garlic and cook, stirring, until the onion begins to soften, 2 to 3 minutes. Be careful not to brown it. Stir in the rice to coat the grains with the fat and onion mixture, and cook about 1 minute longer.

6. ADD the wine and stir until it is mostly absorbed by the rice. Add the broth, ½ cup at time, stirring well after each addition. Wait until each addition of broth is almost completely absorbed before adding the next ½ cup. Reserve ¼ cup of the broth to add at the end.

7. WHEN the rice is tender but firm, in about 20 minutes, turn off the heat. Add the remaining ¼ cup broth and 1 tablespoon butter, the duck meat, squash and mushroom mixture, cheese, sage, parsley, and salt and pepper to taste, and stir well to combine with the rice. Stir in the truffle oil and serve immediately.

3 tablespoons white truffle oil (optional, see Note)

Makes 4 to 6 servings

Note:
Duck *confit*, cooked duck legs, as well as duck foie gras (see page 120) are available by mail order from D'Artagnan, 399-419 St. Paul Avenue, Jersey City, NJ 07306, or telephone, 1-800-DARTAGNAN, as well as from many specialty food and meat stores nationwide.

White truffle oil can be purchased in Italian specialty food stores.

LEEK AND BALSAMIC VINEGAR RISOTTO WITH FRESH DUCK FOIE GRAS

3 tablespoons unsalted butter

1 tablespoon olive oil

2 tablespoons finely chopped shallots

3 medium-size leeks, white parts only, root end discarded, cut in half lengthwise, rinsed, and finely sliced (to yield 2 cups)

2 cups Arborio rice

½ cup dry white wine

6 cups chicken or meat broth, preferably homemade (pages 27–29), heated

1 tablespoon balsamic vinegar

½ cup freshly grated Italian parmesan cheese

2 tablespoons chopped fresh parsley leaves

1 whole Grade A duck foie gras (see Note, page 119), cut lengthwise into ½-inch-thick slices

Salt

Freshly ground black pepper

Makes 4 to 6 servings

Fresh foie gras is one of the richest foods around. It should be cooked quickly in a very hot pan to prevent the luscious duck fat from cooking away. The seared foie gras is served on top of the rice; this refined risotto is the perfect foil for the foie gras.

1. HEAT 2 tablespoons of the butter and the oil in a heavy 4-quart pot over medium-high heat. Add the shallots and leek and cook, stirring, until they begin to soften, 2 to 3 minutes. Be careful not to brown them. Stir in the rice to coat the grains with the fat and leek mixture, and cook about 1 minute longer.

2. ADD the wine and stir until it is mostly absorbed by the rice. Add the broth ½ cup at a time, stirring well after each addition. Wait until each addition of broth is almost completely absorbed before adding the next ½ cup. Reserve ¼ cup of the broth to add at the end.

3. WHEN the rice is tender but firm, in about 20 minutes, turn off the heat. Add the balsamic vinegar, the remaining ¼ cup broth and 1 tablespoon of butter, the cheese, parsley, and salt and pepper to taste, and stir well to combine with the rice.

4. WHILE the risotto is cooking, prepare the foie gras: Place a medium-size heavy skillet over medium-high heat; when it is very hot, add as many of the slices of foie gras as can fit in a single layer and cook quickly until both sides are brown, 1 to 2 minutes on each side. Remove

the foie gras from the skillet, place the pieces on a plate and keep warm until ready to serve. Pour off the fat from the pan and continue cooking until all the slices are done.

5. TO SERVE, spoon the risotto onto warmed dinner plates. Top each serving with slices of the foie gras, and serve immediately.

SWIFT SERVINGS

Always serve risotto as soon as it is finished cooking—preferably on preheated plates or in bowls.

RISOTTO WITH PORCINI AND DUCK LIVERS

1 ounce dried porcini mush-rooms (about ⅔ cup depending on the size of the porcini pieces)

1 cup boiling water

2 tablespoons olive oil

1 pound duck livers, mem-branes and tendons cut away, livers cut into 1-inch pieces

Salt

Freshly ground black pepper

2 tablespoons unsalted butter

½ cup finely chopped onion

2 cups Arborio rice

½ cup dry white wine

6 cups chicken or meat broth, preferably homemade (pages 27–29), heated

½ cup freshly grated Italian parmesan cheese

2 tablespoons chopped fresh parsley leaves, rinsed

Makes 4 to 6 servings

This risotto of porcini and duck livers makes a hearty entrée. Duck livers are available from specialty butchers. You can substitute chicken livers for a more traditional risotto.

1. COMBINE the porcini with the boiling water in a heat-proof 2-cup glass measuring cup. Allow to stand at least 15 minutes. Drain the porcini and finely chop. Strain the soaking liquid, reserve ½ cup, and add it to the broth. Set aside.

2. HEAT 1 tablespoon of the oil in a small skillet over medium-high heat. Add the livers, season with salt and pepper to taste, and cook until brown and cooked through, 7 to 10 minutes. Turn off the heat and set aside.

3. COMBINE the remaining olive oil and 1 tablespoon of the butter in a heavy 4-quart pot over medium-high heat. Add the onion and cook, stirring, until the onion begins to soften, 2 to 3 minutes. Be careful not to brown it. Stir in the rice to coat the grains with the fat and onion mixture, and cook about 1 minute longer.

4. ADD the wine and stir until it is mostly absorbed by the rice. Add the chopped porcini and begin to add the broth, ½ cup at a time, stirring well after each addition. Wait until each addition of broth is almost completely absorbed before adding the next ½ cup. Reserve ¼ cup of the broth to add at the end.

5. WHEN the rice is tender but firm, in about 20 minutes, turn off the heat. Add the remaining ¼ cup broth and the 1 tablespoon butter, the cooked livers, cheese, parsley, and salt and pepper to taste, and stir well to combine with the rice. Serve immediately.

Risotto alla Paella

Paella alla valenciana *is traditionally made with chicken, rabbit, beans, saffron, and land snails; ingredients that have been translated by American cooks, as well as contemporary Spanish cooks, into a surf-and-turf preparation with chicken, sausage, clams, mussels, and usually peas. This risotto recipe is adapted from a paella recipe given to me by my friend Josephina Yanguas, a Cambridge cafe owner and a native of Pamplona. If you can find it, use Valencia rice, a short-grain rice similar to Italian Arborio that is sold in Latin food markets.*

1. HEAT 1 tablespoon of the oil in a large skillet over medium-high heat. Add the chicken, season with salt and pepper to taste, and cook until the pieces are brown, tender, and cooked through, about 8 to 10 minutes.

2. HEAT the remaining 2 tablespoons of the oil in a heavy 4-quart pot over medium-high heat. Add the onion and garlic and cook, stirring, until the onion begins to soften, 2 to 3 minutes. Be careful not to brown it. Stir in the rice to coat the grains with the oil and onion mixture, and cook about 1 minute longer.

3. ADD the paprika, saffron, and the tomatoes and begin to add the broth, ½ cup at a time, stirring well after each addition. Wait until each addition of broth is almost completely absorbed before adding the next ½ cup, stirring frequently to prevent sticking. Reserve ¼ cup of the broth to add at the end.

4. AFTER 15 minutes, stir in the squid and favas. Continue cooking until the rice is tender but firm, and the squid is thoroughly cooked, and turned an opaque white, about 5 minutes longer. Stir in the chicken and parsley. Season with salt and pepper to taste and serve immediately.

3 tablespoons olive oil

1 pound boneless, skinless chicken breast, cut into 1-inch pieces

Salt

Freshly ground black pepper

1 medium-size onion, peeled and chopped

3 large cloves garlic, peeled and pressed or finely chopped

2 cups Valencia or Arborio rice

1 tablespoon hot paprika

Pinch saffron threads (see Box, page 99)

1 cup chopped canned tomatoes, with their juice

6 cups chicken broth, preferably homemade (pages 27–28), heated

8 ounces cleaned squid bodies, sliced into ¼-inch rings

8 ounces fresh fava beans in their pods, shelled and peeled (to yield ½ cup); or ½ cup shelled fresh peas

¼ cup chopped fresh parsley leaves, rinsed

Makes 4 to 6 servings

RISOTTO WITH CHICKEN, LEMONGRASS, AND COCONUT MILK

FOR THE CHICKEN:

1 tablespoon canola, corn, or other vegetable oil

2 tablespoons finely chopped, peeled ginger root

2 large cloves garlic, peeled and pressed or finely chopped

4 scallions, root end discarded, white and green parts chopped separately

1 stalk lemongrass, peeled and finely chopped (bottom 3 inches only)

1 pound boneless, skinless chicken breast, trimmed and sliced into thin strips

FOR THE RISOTTO:

2 tablespoons canola, corn, or other vegetable oil

1 cup finely chopped onion

2 cups American short-grain rice (page 4) or Arborio rice

⅛ teaspoon red pepper flakes, or more to taste

6 cups chicken broth, preferably homemade (pages 27–28), heated

1 cup unsweetened canned coconut milk, well stirred (see Note)

Great eastern flavors make an exotic risotto that's creamy and aromatic. Lemongrass provides a delicate but distinctive taste. To get the best flavor of the lemongrass, cut away the tough top two-thirds of the stalk and peel the remaining lower part of the stalk; the inner stalk is tender and can easily be chopped. Coconut milk is widely available in Asian and Caribbean markets. Be sure to buy only the unsweetened variety. Since coconut milk is an extract made from the coconut meat—not the liquid that you find inside a coconut when you crack it open—it is quite high in fat. You can find low-fat versions that give you the flavor you want in this recipe, although you will lose some of the creaminess. To make this recipe very low-fat, you can add ¼ teaspoon of coconut extract to the risotto and substitute more broth for the coconut milk.

1. PREPARE the chicken: Heat the oil in a small skillet over medium heat. Add the ginger, garlic, scallion whites, and lemongrass and cook, stirring, for about 1 minute. Add the chicken, season with salt to taste, and cook, stirring, until it is mostly cooked through, about 5 minutes. Lower and set aside.

2. PREPARE the risotto: Heat 2 tablespoons of the oil in a heavy 4-quart pot over medium-high heat. Add the onion and cook, stirring, until the onion begins to soften, 2 to 3 minutes. Be careful not to brown it. Stir in the rice and red pepper flakes to coat the grains with the oil and onion mixture, and cook about 1 minute longer.

3. ADD the broth, ½ cup at a time, stirring well after each addition. Wait until each addition of broth is almost

completely absorbed before adding the next ½ cup. Reserve ¼ cup of the broth to add at the end.

4. WHEN the rice is tender but firm, in about 20 minutes, turn off the heat. Add the remaining ¼ cup broth, the coconut milk, nam pla, cilantro, the chicken mixture, and salt and pepper to taste, and stir well to combine with the rice. Spoon the risotto onto warmed dinner plates. Garnish with scallion greens and chopped peanuts. Serve immediately.

2 tablespoons nam pla (Thai fish sauce) (see Note)

2 tablespoons chopped fresh cilantro leaves

Salt

Freshly ground black pepper

⅓ cup coarsely chopped unsalted roasted peanuts

Makes 4 to 6 servings

Note:
Coconut milk and nam pla are available in Asian groceries.

Risotto with Cuban-Style Chicken and Green Peppers

FOR THE CHICKEN:

1 pound boneless, skinless chicken breast, trimmed and sliced into 1-inch-thick strips

2 large cloves garlic, peeled and finely chopped

Juice of 2 limes

2 tablespoons olive oil

¼ teaspoon red pepper flakes, or more to taste

Salt

Freshly ground black pepper

FOR THE RISOTTO:

2 tablespoons olive oil

1 medium-size onion, peeled, cut in half, and sliced into ¼-inch-thick half-rounds

1 large clove garlic, peeled and pressed or finely chopped

1 medium-size green bell pepper, cored, seeded, and chopped

2 cups Arborio rice

½ cup dry white wine

6 cups chicken broth, preferably homemade (page 27–28), heated

Arroz con pollo, the classic Cuban dish, was the inspiration for this recipe.

1. PREPARE the chicken: Combine the chicken with the garlic, half the lime juice, 1 tablespoon of oil, the red pepper flakes, and salt and pepper to taste in a medium-size glass or other nonreactive bowl. Allow to stand at room temperature for 20 minutes.

2. HEAT the remaining tablespoon of oil in a medium-size heavy skillet over medium-high heat. Add the chicken with the marinade and cook, stirring, until the chicken is brown and cooked through, 5 to 7 minutes. Pour the remaining lime juice over the chicken and stir to combine. Remove the skillet from the heat and cover loosely with aluminum foil to keep warm until ready to serve.

3. PREPARE the risotto: Heat the oil in a heavy 4-quart pot over medium-high heat. Add the onion, garlic, and green pepper and cook, stirring, until the onion begins to soften, 2 to 3 minutes. Be careful not to brown it. Stir in the rice to coat the grains with the oil and vegetable mixture, and cook about 1 minute longer.

4. ADD the wine and stir until it is mostly absorbed by the rice. Add the broth, ½ cup at time, stirring well after each addition. Wait until each addition of broth is almost completely absorbed before adding the next ½ cup. Reserve ¼ cup of the broth to add at the end.

5. WHEN the rice is tender but firm, in about 20 minutes, turn off the heat. Add the remaining ¼ cup broth, the cilantro, lime juice, cheese, and salt and pepper and stir well to combine with the rice.

6. TO SERVE, spoon the risotto onto warmed dinner plates. Top each serving with some of the chicken. Serve immediately.

3 tablespoons chopped fresh cilantro leaves

Juice of 1 lime

⅓ cup freshly grated aged asiago cheese (see Box)

Makes 4 to 6 servings

ASIAGO CHEESE

Asiago is a cow's milk cheese, made with partially skimmed milk, from Vicenza in the northeastern Italian region of the Veneto. There are two types of asiago: Asiago d'allevo is the harder of the two cheeses and is typically served as a grating cheese. It has been aged for a year to a year and a half, and has a spicy, savory flavor. Asiago pressato is typically a younger cheese, aged for only about a month, with a pleasantly fresh, slightly sweet taste. It is served as a table cheese.

Risotto with Fennel, Olives, and Orange-Flavored Chicken

FOR THE CHICKEN:

1 tablespoon olive oil

1 pound skinless, boneless chicken breast, trimmed and cut into 2-inch pieces

Salt

Freshly ground black pepper

Juice of ½ orange

1 teaspoon orange oil (optional, see Note)

FOR THE RISOTTO:

2 tablespoons olive oil

½ cup finely chopped onion

1 large clove garlic, peeled and pressed or finely chopped

4 ounces fennel bulb, ribs cut off and discarded, bulb finely chopped (to yield 2 cups)

Zest of ½ orange, cut into fine julienne strips

2 cups Arborio rice

½ cup dry white wine

10 black olives, pitted and cut in half

A zesty risotto with Sicilian flavors that make this dish deliciously piquant. Use a brine-cured black olive—Gaeta or Calamata—for the best taste.

1. PREPARE the chicken: Heat the oil in a medium-size skillet over medium-high heat. Add the chicken, season with salt and pepper to taste, and cook, stirring, until the chicken is well browned on all sides and cooked through, about 10 minutes. Add the orange juice and continue cooking, scraping the browned bits on the bottom of the skillet, until it has been reduced to about 1 tablespoon, 2 to 3 minutes. Pour in the orange oil and stir to combine. Turn off the heat, cover loosely with aluminum foil to keep warm, and set aside.

2. PREPARE the risotto: Heat the oil in a heavy 4-quart pot over medium-high heat. Add the onion, garlic, fennel, and orange zest and cook, stirring, until the vegetables begin to soften, 2 to 3 minutes. Be careful not to brown them. Stir in the rice to coat the grains with the oil and vegetable mixture, and cook about 1 minute longer.

3. ADD the wine and stir until it is mostly absorbed by the rice. Add the olives; begin to add the broth, ½ cup at a time, stirring well after each addition. Wait until each addition of broth is almost completely absorbed before adding the next ½ cup. Reserve ¼ cup of the broth to add at the end.

4. WHEN the rice is tender but firm, in about 20 minutes, turn off the heat. Add the remaining ¼ cup broth, cheese, basil, and salt and pepper to taste, and stir to combine with the rice.

5. SPOON the risotto onto warmed dinner plates. Garnish with the chicken and serve immediately.

6 cups chicken broth, preferably homemade (pages 27–28), heated

⅓ cup freshly grated Pecorino cheese

¼ cup chopped fresh basil leaves

Makes 4 to 6 servings

Note:
Flavored oils of all varieties are available in specialty food stores. A particularly good orange oil is made by Boyajian.

Risotto with Chicken, Figs, and Pignoli

3 tablespoons olive oil

1 pound boneless, skinless chicken breast, trimmed and cut into 1-inch pieces

Salt

Freshly ground black pepper

⅓ cup Armagnac or dry white wine

1 medium-size onion, peeled, cut in half, and thinly sliced (to yield 2 cups)

2 pinches granulated sugar

3 large cloves garlic, peeled and pressed or finely chopped

2 cups Arborio rice

½ teaspoon fennel seed

½ cup dry white wine

6 cups chicken broth, preferably homemade (pages 27–28), heated

1 cup stemmed and chopped dried figs (about 6 whole figs)

¼ cup freshly grated Italian parmesan cheese

2 tablespoons chopped fresh parsley leaves, rinsed

2 tablespoons pine nuts (pignoli), toasted

Makes 4 to 6 servings

This is a savory, rustic risotto with great flavors.

1. In a small skillet, heat 1 tablespoon of oil over medium-high heat. Add the chicken, season with salt and pepper to taste, and cook, stirring, until brown, 2 to 3 minutes. Add the Armagnac and continue cooking, while stirring, until the chicken is cooked through and the Armagnac has been reduced to about 2 tablespoons, about 8 minutes longer. Turn off the heat, cover loosely with aluminum foil to keep warm and set aside.

2. Heat the remaining 2 tablespoons of the oil in a heavy 4-quart pot over medium-high heat. Add the onion and sugar and cook, stirring, until the onions are brown, about 10 minutes. Add the garlic and fennel seed. Stir in the rice to coat the grains with the onion and oil mixture, and cook about 1 minute longer.

3. Add the wine and stir until it is mostly absorbed by the rice. Add the broth, ½ cup at a time, stirring well after each addition. Wait until each addition of broth is almost completely absorbed before adding the next ½ cup. Reserve ¼ cup of the broth to add at the end.

4. When the rice is tender but firm, in about 20 minutes, turn off the heat. Add the remaining ¼ cup broth, the chicken, figs, cheese, parsley, pine nuts, and salt and pepper to taste, and stir well to combine with the rice. Serve immediately.

RISOTTO WITH SMOKED TURKEY SAUSAGE AND SUN-DRIED TOMATOES

Aidell's sausages are some of the best all-natural sausages you can buy. I am particularly fond of the smoked chicken and turkey sausage and have found it gives risotto a deliciously piquant taste, especially when combined with sun-dried tomatoes. If you are using dry tomatoes that haven't been packed in oil, be sure to plump them in boiling water before adding them to the recipe and substitute olive oil for the tomato oil.

1. COMBINE the sun-dried tomatoes, parsley, and the sun-dried tomato oil in the bowl of a food processor and process 30 seconds until the mixture is finely chopped (or chop by hand). Set aside.

2. HEAT the olive oil with the butter in a heavy 4-quart pot over medium-high heat. Add the onion and cook, stirring, until the onion begins to soften, 2 to 3 minutes. Be careful not to brown it. Stir in the rice to coat the grains with the fat and onion mixture, and cook about 1 minute longer.

3. ADD the sliced sausage pieces and begin to add the broth, ½ cup at a time, stirring well after each addition. Wait until each addition of broth is almost completely absorbed by the rice before adding the next ½ cup. Reserve ¼ cup of the broth to add at the end.

4. WHEN the rice is tender but firm, in about 20 minutes, turn off the heat. Add the remaining ¼ cup broth, the cheese, the sun-dried tomato mixture, and salt and pepper to taste. Stir well to combine with the rice. Serve immediately.

½ cup sun-dried tomato halves packed in oil

¼ cup fresh parsley leaves, rinsed

1 tablespoon oil in which the sun-dried tomatoes were packed, or substitute plain olive oil

1 tablespoon olive oil

1 tablespoon unsalted butter

½ cup finely chopped onion

2 cups Arborio rice

8 ounces turkey sausage, cut crosswise into ½-inch-thick slices

6 cups chicken broth, preferably homemade (pages 27–28), heated

½ cup freshly grated Italian parmesan cheese

Salt

Freshly ground black pepper

Makes 4 to 6 servings

Sweet Potato and Cilantro Risotto with Turkey

2 tablespoons olive oil

½ cup finely chopped onion

1 clove garlic, peeled and pressed or finely chopped

2 cups Arborio rice

½ cup dry white wine

1 medium-size sweet potato or yam (about 8 ounces), peeled and diced (to yield 1 ½ cups)

6 cups chicken broth, preferably homemade (pages 27–28), heated

⅓ cup freshly grated Italian parmesan cheese

⅓ cup chopped fresh cilantro leaves

¼ cup chopped fresh parsley leaves, rinsed

2 tablespoons lime juice

8 ounces cooked turkey, shredded, at room temperature

Salt

Freshly ground black pepper

Makes 4 to 6 servings

These New World ingredients make a flavorful risotto. You can use smoked or roasted store-bought turkey breast or you can use leftover home-cooked turkey meat. Either way, it makes this a quick and easy meal.

1. HEAT the oil in a heavy 4-quart pot over medium-high heat. Add the onion and garlic and cook, stirring, until the onion begins to soften, 2 to 3 minutes. Be careful not to brown it. Stir in the rice to coat the grains with the oil and onion mixture, and cook about 1 minute longer.

2. ADD the wine and stir until it is mostly absorbed by the rice. Stir in the potato and begin to add the broth, ½ cup at a time, stirring well after each addition. Wait until each addition of broth is almost completely absorbed before adding the next ½ cup. Reserve ¼ cup of the broth to add at the end.

3. WHEN the rice is tender but firm, in about 20 minutes, turn off the heat. Add the remaining ¼ cup broth, the cheese, cilantro, parsley, lime juice, and salt and pepper to taste, and stir well to combine.

4. SERVE the risotto on warmed dinner plates. Top each serving with some of the turkey. Serve immediately.

chapter SEVEN

Low-Fat Risotti

$\mathcal{T}$here's no question that butter and cheese add flavor and richness to risotto and are mostly responsible for the luxurious creamy consistency associated with this dish. But it is possible to make risotto with a lot less fat than is traditionally called for without completely compromising the taste and texture.

In fact, risotto is one of the best and easiest low-fat dishes you can prepare. With as little as a single tablespoon of oil, you can make an uncompromisingly flavorful and satisfying risotto that comes close to being every bit as thick, rich, and creamy as a traditional risotto made with more added fat.

Low-fat risotto doesn't require any cooking tricks or special ingredients, only a few simple changes in the traditional recipe:

- As with most low-fat cooking, a pot with a nonstick surface is advisable (you should also use skillets with nonstick surfaces if you are sautéing). The nonstick surface prevents the onions, initially, and then the rice from sticking to the pot. It also makes the cleanup easier.

- Use the traditional classic stand-and-stir risotto technique for preparing low-fat risotto. It is the gradual addition of broth that helps to give the finished dish its creamy, smooth texture so you won't miss the enriching ingredients, butter and cheeses, in the risotto.

- One tablespoon of oil is enough to start the risotto: to sauté the onions and the rice before adding wine and broth. One tablespoon of oil, in recipes for 4 to 6 servings, means that there is hardly a half-teaspoon of oil per serving. However, you can reduce the amount of oil even more if you wish. One Italian I know, who cannot tolerate any fat in his diet, prepares his risotto with no oil; he cooks the onion in stock instead.

- Use defatted broth (see recipes on pages 27–31) to ensure your risotto is as low-fat as possible. Defatting can be accomplished easily: After cooking the broth, strain it; allow the broth to cool completely and chill overnight. Any fat in the broth will collect and harden on the surface. Use a large spoon to remove the fat from the broth. If you use canned broth, chill it before using to remove excess fat. Check the label and fat content on bouillon cube packages and select a brand with a low-fat content.

- In following the recipes, if you want to improvise and add different ingredients, be sure to add ingredients that are low in fat rather than higher-fat meats or cheeses.

- Most of the recipes call for 2 tablespoons of parmesan cheese to be added to the risotto at the end of the cooking process. Each tablespoon of parmesan contains 23 calories and 2 grams of fat (source: *The Fat Counter*, Natow and Heslin, PocketBooks, 1989). The cheese adds flavor and works to lightly thicken the sauce around the rice. However, you can reduce or eliminate the cheese in each recipe.

- All of these recipes can also be prepared in the traditional manner. Add a tablespoon of butter when you begin to cook the risotto, and one at the end when the risotto is finished. Increase the amount of parmesan cheese to ⅓ cup.

Low-Fat Porcini Mushroom Risotto

1 ounce dried porcini mushrooms (about ⅔ cup,
  depending on the size of the
  porcini)

1 cup boiling water

1 tablespoon olive oil

½ cup finely chopped onion

2 cups Arborio rice

½ cup dry white wine

5 cups defatted chicken broth,
  preferably homemade (pages
  27–28), heated

2 tablespoons freshly grated
  Italian parmesan cheese

Salt

Freshly ground black pepper

Makes 4 to 6 servings

This is a low-fat variation on a classic Italian recipe. Be sure to combine the liquid in which the dry mushrooms were soaked with the broth. The mushroom-soaking liquid adds lots of mushroom flavor and gives this risotto its distinctive character.

1. COMBINE the porcini with the boiling water in a heat-proof 2-cup glass measuring cup. Allow to stand at least 15 minutes. Drain the porcini and finely chop. Strain the soaking liquid, reserve ½ cup of it, and add it to the broth. Set aside.

2. HEAT the oil in a heavy 4-quart pot over medium-high heat. Add the onion and cook, stirring, until it begins to soften, 2 to 3 minutes. Be careful not to brown it. Stir in the rice to coat the grains with the oil and onion, and cook about 1 minute longer.

3. ADD the wine and stir until it is mostly absorbed by the rice. Add the porcini and begin to add the broth, ½ cup at a time, stirring well after each addition. Wait until each addition is almost completely absorbed before adding the next ½ cup. Reserve ¼ cup of the broth to add at the end.

4. WHEN the rice is tender but firm, in about 20 minutes, turn off the heat. Add the remaining ¼ cup broth, the cheese, and salt and pepper to taste, and stir well to combine. Serve immediately.

Low-Fat Lemon and Asparagus Risotto

This is a lemony risotto with the great fresh flavor of asparagus.

1. HEAT the oil in a heavy 4-quart pot over medium-high heat. Add the shallots and cook, stirring, until the shallots begin to soften, 2 to 3 minutes. Be careful not to brown them. Stir in the rice to coat the grains with the oil and shallot mixture, and cook about 1 minute longer. Add the lemon zest and 2 tablespoons of the lemon juice and stir until it is mostly absorbed by the rice.

2. ADD the broth, ½ cup at a time, stirring well after each addition. Wait until each addition is almost completely absorbed before adding the next ½ cup. Reserve ¼ cup of the broth to add at the end. After 15 minutes add the asparagus.

3. WHEN the rice is tender but firm, about 5 minutes longer, turn off the heat. Add the remaining ¼ cup broth, 1 tablespoon of lemon juice, the parmesan, salt and pepper to taste, and stir well to combine with the rice. Serve immediately.

1 tablespoon olive oil

⅓ cup finely chopped shallots

2 cups Arborio rice

1 large lemon, zest grated and juiced (about 4 tablespoons lemon juice)

6 cups defatted chicken broth, preferably homemade (pages 27–28), heated

1 pound fresh asparagus spears, tough bottoms discarded, spears peeled and finely chopped

1 tablespoon freshly grated Italian parmesan cheese

Salt

Freshly ground black pepper

Makes 4 to 6 servings

LOW-FAT SHELLFISH RISOTTO

18 littleneck clams in the shell, rinsed

24 mussels in the shell, bearded and rinsed just before cooking

1 cup cold water

1 tablespoon olive oil

½ cup finely chopped onion

½ cup chopped canned tomatoes, with their juice

1 cup Arborio rice

½ cup dry white wine

5 cups defatted chicken broth or fish broth, preferably homemade (pages 27–28 and 32–33), heated

8 ounces medium-size raw shrimp, peeled and deveined, finely chopped

¼ cup chopped fresh parsley leaves, rinsed

Makes 4 to 6 servings

With lots of shellfish, this is a very flavorful and filling dish.

1. COMBINE the clams and mussels with the water in a 4-quart saucepan with a tight-fitting lid. Cover and place over medium-high heat. Cook until the shells are open, 7 to 10 minutes. Discard any clams or mussels with unopened shells. Reserve 6 whole clams and 12 mussels, in their shells, as a garnish. Remove the remaining shellfish from their shells; rinse under warm water to remove any residual sand, drain and chop. Set aside.

2. HEAT the oil in a heavy 4-quart pot over medium-high heat. Add the onion and cook, stirring, until it begins to soften, 2 to 3 minutes. Be careful not to brown it. Add the tomatoes and stir to combine with the onion. Stir in the rice to coat the grains with the tomato and onion mixture, and cook about 1 minute longer.

3. ADD the wine and stir until it is mostly absorbed by the rice. Add the broth, ½ cup at a time, stirring well after each addition. Wait until each addition is almost completely absorbed before adding the next ½ cup. Reserve ¼ cup of the broth to add at the end. After 15 minutes stir in the shellfish.

4. WHEN the rice is tender but firm, about 5 minutes longer, turn off the heat. Stir in the remaining ¼ cup broth and the parsley and serve immediately. Garnish each serving with the reserved whole clams and mussels.

LOW-FAT RADICCHIO AND SWISS CHARD RISOTTO

The colorful contrast of the red radicchio and the deep green of the chard make a striking risotto with a refreshing taste. Use a vegetable broth to make this elegant main course vegetarian, or use chicken broth.

1. HEAT the oil in a heavy 4-quart pot over medium-high heat. Add the shallots and cook, stirring, until the shallots begin to soften, 1 to 2 minutes. Be careful not to brown them. Stir in the rice to coat the grains with the oil and shallot mixture, and cook about 1 minute longer.

2. ADD the wine and stir until it is mostly absorbed by the rice. Add the radicchio and begin to add the broth, ½ cup at a time, stirring well after each addition. Wait until each addition is almost completely absorbed before adding the next ½ cup. Reserve ¼ cup of the broth to add at the end. After 15 minutes, stir in the Swiss chard.

3. WHEN the rice is tender but firm, about 5 minutes longer, turn off the heat. Add the remaining ¼ cup broth, the cheese, and salt and pepper to taste, and stir well to combine. Serve immediately.

1 tablespoon olive oil

½ cup finely chopped shallots

2 cups Arborio rice

½ cup dry white wine

8 ounces radicchio, shredded (to yield about 4 cups)

6 cups defatted vegetable broth, preferably homemade (pages 30–31, heated

1 bunch (1 ½ to 2 pounds) green Swiss chard, ribs cut out and reserved for another use, leaves roughly chopped (to yield 3 cups)

2 tablespoons freshly grated Italian parmesan cheese

Salt

Freshly ground black pepper

Makes 4 to 6 servings

LOW-FAT SHRIMP AND ARTICHOKE RISOTTO

2 medium-size artichokes
(about 1 pound total)

1 lemon, juiced (to yield
3 to 4 tablespoons)

Salt

Freshly ground black pepper

1 tablespoon olive oil

½ cup finely chopped shallots

2 cups Arborio rice

½ cup dry white wine

6 cups defatted chicken broth,
preferably homemade (pages
27–28), heated

8 ounces medium-size raw
shrimp, peeled, deveined,
and chopped

2 tablespoons chopped fresh
parsley leaves, rinsed

Makes 4 to 6 servings

This is a low-fat variation on a risotto I enjoyed in La Scudderia, one of the best restaurants of Palermo, Sicily. The artichokes are cooked separately with lots of lemon and added to the risotto at the end.

1. PREPARE the artichokes: Cut the stems, leaving about 1 inch from the base. Pull off the tough, dark green leaves, starting with the leaves closest to the stem, until only the yellow-green leaves are visible. Do not use a scissors or knife for this; the leaves will break naturally at the point where the tough part ends and the tender part begins. Using a serrated knife, cut 2 inches off the top of the artichoke, peel the stem, and trim around the base of the artichoke. Cut the artichoke into quarters lengthwise. Cut out the fuzzy choke from each quarter and the spiky sharp leaves just above it. Thinly slice the artichoke bottoms and chop to yield approximately 2 cups.

2. PLACE the artichoke pieces in a small saucepan with the lemon juice, salt to taste, and just enough water to cover. Place over medium-high heat and bring the liquid to a boil. Cover the pan, reduce the heat to low, and cook until the artichokes are tender and the liquid has mostly cooked away, about 20 minutes. Turn off the heat and set aside, covered, to keep warm.

3. HEAT the oil in a heavy 4-quart pot over medium-high heat. Add the shallots and cook, stirring, until the shallots begin to soften, 2 to 3 minutes. Be careful not to brown them. Stir in the rice to coat the grains with the oil and shallot mixture, and cook about 1 minute longer.

4. ADD the wine and stir until it is mostly absorbed by the rice. Add the broth, ½ cup at a time, stirring well after each addition. Wait until each addition is almost completely absorbed before adding the next ½ cup. Reserve ¼ cup of the broth to add at the end. After 15 minutes stir in the shrimp.

5. WHEN the rice is tender but firm, about 5 minutes longer, turn off the heat. Add the remaining ¼ cup broth, the artichokes, parsley, and salt and pepper to taste, and stir well to combine with the rice.

Low-Fat Risotto with Black Mushrooms, Broccoli, and Steamed Shredded Chicken

1 ounce dried Chinese black mushrooms (about 1 cup)

1 cup boiling water

5 cups defatted Chinese Chicken Broth (page 28), heated

1 whole boneless, skinless chicken breast (about 1 pound), trimmed

2 ¼-inch-thick slices fresh peeled ginger root

¼ cup rice wine (sake)

2 tablespoons corn, canola oil, or other vegetable oil

1 tablespoon finely chopped or grated peeled ginger root

1 scallion, root end discarded, finely chopped

2 large cloves garlic, peeled and pressed or finely chopped

2 cups Chinese rice (page 4) or Arborio rice

½ cup rice wine (sake)

2 cups broccoli florets

1 bunch fresh watercress, rinsed and dried, thickest stems discarded, very finely chopped preferably in a food processor

This Chinese-flavored risotto has good strong flavors that make a satisfyingly robust main-course dish. Use American-Chinese rice or Arborio; both work equally well in this recipe.

1. COMBINE the mushrooms with the boiling water in a small heatproof bowl and allow to stand 30 minutes. Drain the mushrooms, reserving the soaking liquid, and finely chop. Combine the soaking liquid with the Chinese Chicken Broth in a medium-size saucepan over medium heat, and simmer 10 minutes before adding to the risotto.

2. PREPARE the chicken: Combine the chicken with the ginger, rice wine, and salt on a plate and place in a steamer basket over boiling water. Steam, covered, until the chicken is cooked through, about 10 minutes (or place chicken on a microwave-safe plate with flavorings, cover securely with microwave-safe paper or plastic, and cook in the microwave until done, about 5 minutes). Slice the chicken breast lengthwise into thin strips. Cover to keep warm, and set aside.

3. HEAT the oil in a heavy 4-quart pot over medium-high heat. Add the ginger, scallion, and garlic and cook about 1 minute. Be careful not to brown them. Stir in the rice to coat the grains with the oil and ginger mixture, and cook about 1 minute longer.

4. ADD the rice wine and cook until it is mostly absorbed by the rice. Add the broth, ½ cup at a time, stirring well after each addition. Wait until each addition is almost

completely absorbed before adding the next ½ cup. Reserve ¼ cup of the broth to add at the end. When the rice has been cooking 15 minutes, stir in the broccoli.

5. WHEN the rice is tender but firm, about 5 minutes longer, turn off the heat. Add the remaining ¼ cup broth, the watercress, and salt and pepper to taste, and stir well to combine. Serve the risotto with the chicken pieces on top, as a garnish. Serve immediately.

Salt

Freshly ground black pepper

Makes 4 to 6 servings

Low-Fat Parsnip and Butternut Squash Risotto with Herbs

1 tablespoon olive oil

½ cup finely chopped onion

2 small parsnips (about 4 ounces) total, tops trimmed, peeled and chopped

2 cups Arborio rice

½ cup dry white wine

6 cups defatted chicken broth, preferably homemade (pages 27–28), heated

1 cup shredded, peeled, and seeded butternut squash

2 tablespoons chopped mixed fresh herbs such as basil, mint, sage, chives, and parsley; or 2 teaspoons dried

2 tablespoons freshly grated Italian parmesan cheese

Salt

Freshly ground black pepper

Makes 4 to 6 servings

A perfect risotto to prepare in the fall or winter. Use fresh herbs if you can find them, but dry herbs also work well in this dish.

1. HEAT the oil in a heavy 4-quart pot over medium-high heat. Add the onion and parsnips and cook, stirring, until the onion begins to soften, 2 to 3 minutes. Be careful not to brown it. Stir in the rice to coat the grains with the oil and onion mixture, and cook about 1 minute longer.

2. ADD the wine and stir until it is mostly absorbed by the rice. Add the broth, ½ cup at a time, stirring well after each addition. Wait until each addition is almost completely absorbed before adding the next ½ cup. Reserve ¼ cup of the broth to add at the end. After 10 minutes add the butternut squash.

3. WHEN the rice is tender but firm, about 10 minutes longer, turn off the heat. Add the remaining ¼ cup broth, the herbs, cheese, salt and pepper to taste, and stir well to combine with the rice.

LOW-FAT RISOTTO WITH WHITE BEANS AND KALE

This risotto makes a satisfying main-course dish with its healthful components of vegetable protein, simple and complex carbohydrates, and little added fat.

1. HEAT the oil in a heavy 4-quart pot over medium-high heat. Add the onion and garlic and cook, stirring, until the onion begins to soften, 2 to 3 minutes. Be careful not to brown it. Stir in the rice to coat the grains with the oil and onion mixture, and cook about 1 minute longer.

2. ADD the wine and stir until it is mostly absorbed by the rice. Add the broth, ½ cup at a time, stirring well after each addition. Wait until each addition is almost completely absorbed before adding the next ½ cup. Reserve ¼ cup of the broth to add at the end. After 15 minutes add the kale.

3. WHEN the rice is tender but firm, about 5 minutes longer, turn off the heat. Add the remaining ¼ cup broth, the beans, cheese, and salt and pepper to taste, and stir well to combine with the rice.

1 tablespoon olive oil

1 cup finely chopped onion

1 large clove garlic, peeled and pressed or finely chopped

2 cups Arborio rice

½ cup dry white wine

6 cups defatted chicken broth or vegetable broth, preferably homemade (pages 27–28 and 30–31), heated

3 cups fresh kale leaves, ribs removed, rinsed, dried, and coarsely chopped (to yield about 1 ½ cups)

1 cup cooked small white beans such as Great Northern, navy, or white kidney, rinsed and drained if canned

2 tablespoons freshly grated Italian parmesan cheese

Salt

Freshly ground black pepper

Makes 4 to 6 servings

Low-Fat Risotto with Fennel and Broccoli

8 ounces broccoli, stem peeled, trimmed, and cut into 2-inch pieces, florets cut into small individual pieces

8 ounces fennel bulb, ribs and leaves cut off and discarded, trimmed and cut into 2-inch pieces

1 cup water

1 tablespoon olive oil

½ cup finely chopped onion

2 cups Arborio rice

½ cup dry white wine

6 cups defatted chicken broth, preferably homemade (pages 27–28), heated

¼ cup chopped fresh parsley leaves, rinsed

2 tablespoons freshly grated Italian parmesan cheese

Salt

Freshly ground black pepper

Makes 4 to 6 servings

The flavor of fresh fennel becomes subdued when it's cooked. This mild anise taste blends beautifully with the broccoli in a creamy purée to make a fine risotto with a pale green color.

1. COMBINE the broccoli and fennel in a small saucepan with the water and place over medium-high heat. When the water comes to a boil, reduce the heat to medium-low, cover the saucepan, and cook about 15 minutes until the vegetables are tender when pierced with a sharp knife. Transfer the vegetables with the liquid to the work bowl of a food processor or blender and purée the mixture (you should have about 2 cups). Set aside.

2. HEAT the oil in a heavy 4-quart pot over medium-high heat. Add the onion and cook, stirring, until the onion begins to soften, 2 to 3 minutes. Be careful not to brown it. Stir in the rice to coat the grains with the oil and onion mixture, and cook about 1 minute longer.

3. ADD the wine and stir until it is mostly absorbed by the rice. Add the broth, ½ cup at a time, stirring well after each addition. Wait until each addition is almost completely absorbed before adding the next ½ cup. Reserve ¼ cup of the broth to add at the end.

4. WHEN the rice is tender but firm, in about 20 minutes, turn off the heat. Add the remaining ¼ cup broth, the broccoli and fennel purée, the parsley, cheese, and salt and pepper to taste, and stir well to combine with the rice.

LOW-FAT RISOTTO WITH ZUCCHINI, YELLOW SUMMER SQUASH, AND BASIL

Flavorful and colorful, this is my favorite risotto to make in August when squash and basil are most plentiful and most delicious.

1. HEAT the oil in a heavy 4-quart pot over medium-high heat. Add the onion and garlic and cook, stirring, until the onion begins to soften, 2 to 3 minutes. Be careful not to brown it. Stir in the rice to coat the grains with the oil and onion mixture, and cook about 1 minute longer.

2. ADD the wine and stir until it is mostly absorbed by the rice. Add the broth, ½ cup at a time, stirring well after each addition. Wait until each addition is almost completely absorbed before adding the next ½ cup. Reserve ¼ cup of the broth to add at the end. After 15 minutes stir in the zucchini and squash.

3. WHEN the rice is tender but firm, about 5 minutes longer, turn off the heat. Add the remaining ¼ cup broth, the cheese, basil, and salt and pepper to taste, and stir well to combine with the rice.

1 tablespoon olive oil

½ cup finely chopped onion

1 large clove garlic, peeled and pressed or finely chopped

2 cups Arborio rice

½ cup dry white wine

6 cups defatted chicken broth, preferably homemade (pages 27–28), heated

8 ounces zucchini, ends trimmed, cut into julienne strips

8 ounces yellow summer squash, ends trimmed, cut into julienne strips

2 tablespoons freshly grated Italian parmesan cheese

¼ cup chopped fresh basil leaves

Salt

Freshly ground black pepper

Makes 4 to 6 servings

Low-Fat Yellow Beet and Arugula Risotto

2 medium-size yellow beets, about 8 ounces total

1 tablespoon olive oil

½ cup chopped onion

2 cups Arborio rice

½ cup dry white wine

6 cups defatted vegetable broth, preferably homemade (pages 30–31), heated

1 bunch arugula, stems cut off and discarded, leaves rinsed in several changes of cold water, spun dry and finely chopped (to yield 1 cup)

2 tablespoons freshly grated Italian parmesan cheese

Salt

Freshly ground black pepper

Makes 4 to 6 servings

The contrast in flavors—sweet beets and sharp, bitter arugula—makes a savory play on your palate. Yellow beets are more mildly flavored than their red relative and have the added advantage of not coloring the rice as they cook. Since they are a specialty produce item, and may not be easily available, good substitutes include carrots, yams, or even yellow turnip. You can substitute watercress for the arugula.

1. PUT the beets in a small saucepan with water to cover. Place over medium-high heat and bring the water to a boil. Reduce the heat to low and cook about 30 minutes until the beets are tender when pierced with a sharp knife. Drain and allow to cool until you can handle them. Peel the beets and dice to yield 1 ½ cups.

2. HEAT the oil in a heavy 4-quart pot over medium-high heat. Add the onion and cook, stirring, until the onion begins to soften, 2 to 3 minutes. Be careful not to brown it. Stir in the rice to coat the grains with the oil and onion mixture, and cook about 1 minute longer.

3. ADD the wine and stir until it is mostly absorbed by the rice. Add the broth, ½ cup at a time, stirring well after each addition. Wait until each addition is almost completely absorbed before adding the next ½ cup. Reserve ¼ cup of the broth to add at the end.

4. WHEN the rice is tender but firm, in about 20 minutes, turn off the heat. Add the remaining ¼ cup broth, the arugula, beets, cheese, and salt and pepper to taste, and stir well to combine with the rice. Serve immediately.

LOW-FAT VERY GREEN RISOTTO

Spinach makes this an intensely bright green dish. The refreshing taste makes a wonderful first course, whether or not you are on a low-fat diet. You can use either fresh or frozen spinach.

1. PLACE the spinach in the bowl of a food processor and process until the leaves are finely chopped, or chop by hand. Set aside.

2. HEAT the oil in a heavy 4-quart pot over medium-high heat. Add the onion and garlic and cook, stirring, 2 to 3 minutes until the onions begin to soften. Be careful not to brown it. Stir in the rice to coat the grains with the oil and onion mixture, and cook about 1 minute longer.

3. ADD the wine and stir until it is mostly absorbed by the rice. Add the broth, ½ cup at a time, stirring well after each addition. Wait until each addition is almost completely absorbed before adding the next ½ cup. Reserve ¼ cup of the broth to add at the end. After 15 minutes, stir in the spinach.

4. WHEN the rice is tender but firm, about 5 minutes longer, turn off the heat. Add the remaining ¼ cup broth and the cheese, salt and pepper to taste, and stir well to combine with the rice. Serve immediately.

4 cups packed fresh spinach leaves, rinsed, stemmed, and dried; or one 10-ounce package frozen chopped spinach, cooked according to the directions on the package and drained to remove as much water as possible

1 tablespoon olive oil

1 large clove garlic, peeled and pressed or finely chopped

½ cup finely chopped onion

2 cups Arborio rice

½ cup dry white wine

6 cups defatted chicken broth, preferably homemade (pages 27–28), heated

2 tablespoons freshly grated Italian parmesan cheese

Salt

Freshly ground black pepper

Makes 4 to 6 servings

LOW-FAT CHERRY TOMATO RISOTTO WITH FRESH BASIL

1 tablespoon olive oil

½ cup chopped onion

1 large clove garlic, peeled and pressed

1 pound ripe red cherry tomatoes (about 1 ½ pints), seeded

2 cups Arborio rice

6 cups defatted chicken broth, preferably homemade (pages 27–28), heated

¼ cup chopped fresh basil leaves

4 ounces fresh mozzarella, coarsely chopped (to yield about 1 cup) (optional)

Salt

Freshly ground black pepper

2 tablespoons freshly grated Italian parmesan cheese (optional)

Makes 4 to 6 servings

The idea for this recipe was given to me by Romano Tamani, a flamboyant, extraordinary chef and owner of the restaurant L'Ambasciatta in Quistello in Italy.

Use only very ripe cherry tomatoes, preferably in the summer when they're at their best and most flavorful. Because the tomatoes are added whole, the risotto is cumbersome to stir at first, but as the risotto cooks, the tomatoes break apart and create an unusually flavorful dish.

I have listed fresh mozzarella as an optional ingredient. It adds more fat to the risotto, but it also makes a richer, creamier dish.

1. HEAT the oil in a heavy 4-quart pot over medium-high heat. Add the onion, garlic, and tomatoes and cook, stirring, until the onion begins to soften, 2 to 3 minutes. Be careful not to brown it. Stir in the rice to coat the grains with the oil and onion mixture, and cook about 1 minute longer.

2. GRADUALLY add the broth, ½ cup at a time, stirring well after each addition. Wait until each addition is almost completely absorbed before adding the next ½ cup. Reserve ¼ cup of the broth to add at the end.

3. WHEN the rice is tender but firm, in about 20 minutes, turn off the heat. Add the remaining ¼ cup broth, basil, the mozzarella if you are using it, and salt and pepper to taste, and stir well to combine the ingredients. Serve immediately with a sprinkling of parmesan cheese.

chapter EIGHT

Risotto Cakes

To Italians, risotto cakes are *risotto al salto*, risotto "with a jump," because the cake is flipped during cooking. They were invented in restaurants in Milan for pre- and post-theater diners who were in too much of a hurry to wait for the classic preparation. One of the first fast foods, *risotto al salto*, was traditionally formed from cooked, chilled *risotto alla milanese*, saffron risotto, fried in butter and served with only a sprinkling of freshly grated parmigiano-reggiano cheese.

Just as risotto has become a diverse dish made with ingredients as varied as the chefs who prepare it, risotto cakes, at least in the U.S., have also taken on an array of flavors since they were first prepared in Milan. Today's risotto cakes can be made with just about any risotto, and served as a first or main course, or as the accompaniment to meat, chicken, or fish.

What makes risotto cakes so appealing is that they are a wonderful way to serve and enjoy risotto without standing over a simmering pot. You can cook the risotto in advance—hours or even a day—and form the cakes and pan fry them just before serving.

Risotto cakes are also a tasteful way to use up leftover risotto, but if you want to serve them to guests, and have enough to go around, you'll probably need to prepare the risotto specially in advance.

Basic Recipe for Risotto Cakes

1. COMBINE 1 tablespoon of the oil with the butter in a heavy 2- to 3-quart saucepan over medium-high heat. Add the onion and cook, stirring, until the onion begins to soften, 2 to 3 minutes. Be careful not to brown it. Stir in the rice to coat the grains with the fat and onion mixture, and cook about 1 minute longer.

2. MEANWHILE heat 2½ cups of broth in a saucepan over medium heat. When the broth is hot, add 2 cups to the rice, reduce the heat to low, cover the saucepan, and cook exactly 15 minutes. Turn off the heat.

3. UNCOVER the pan, add the remaining ½ cup broth, the cheese, and salt and pepper to taste, and stir to combine with the rice. Allow to cool completely and refrigerate, covered, at least 3 hours or overnight.

4. WHEN the risotto is cold, form the chilled risotto into patty-shaped cakes with your hands, using approximately ½ cup of cooked risotto for each cake. (Make 6 smaller cakes to serve 6, or 4 larger cakes to serve 4.) Compress the cakes, as you form them, as much as possible to reduce the possibility of the cakes falling apart during cooking.

5. OVER medium-high heat, heat 2 to 3 tablespoons of oil in a 10-inch skillet, preferably one with a nonstick surface (if the skillet has an uncoated surface, you'll have to add enough oil to completely cover the bottom). Add the cakes, as many as will fit in the skillet without touching one another, and cook approximately 10 minutes on each side until brown. Serve immediately.

About ¼ cup olive oil

1 tablespoon unsalted butter

⅓ cup finely chopped onion

1 cup Arborio rice

2 ½ cups chicken broth, preferably homemade (pages 27–28), heated

½ cup freshly grated Italian parmesan cheese

Salt

Freshly ground black pepper

Makes 4 to 6 servings

Gorgonzola Risotto Cakes with Portobello Mushrooms

1 tablespoon unsalted butter

About ½ cup olive oil

¼ cup finely chopped shallots

1 cup Arborio rice

2 ½ cups chicken broth, preferably homemade (pages 27–28), heated

2 pounds portobello, shiitake, or crimini mushrooms, stemmed and finely sliced

Salt

Freshly ground black pepper

2 ounces Italian gorgonzola cheese

½ cup freshly grated Italian parmesan cheese

Makes 4 to 6 servings

These risotto cakes make a hearty, satisfying vegetarian entrée for dinner. The forceful gorgonzola cheese is complemented by the earthy taste of the portobello mushrooms.

1. COMBINE the butter and 1 tablespoon of oil in a medium-size, 2- to 3-quart, heavy saucepan with a tight-fitting lid over medium-high heat. Add the shallots and cook, stirring, until the shallots begin to soften, 2 to 3 minutes. Be careful not to brown them. Stir in the rice to coat the grains with the fat and shallot mixture, and cook about 1 minute longer.

2. ADD 2 cups of the broth, reduce the heat to low, cover the saucepan, and cook until the rice is tender but firm, exactly 15 minutes. Turn off the heat.

3. Uncover the pan, add the remaining ½ cup of broth, the gorgonzola, parmesan, and salt and pepper to taste, and stir to combine with the rice. Allow the risotto to cool to room temperature. Refrigerate, covered, until the risotto is completely chilled, at least 3 hours.

4. WHEN the risotto is cold, form into small patty-shaped cakes, using about ½ cup of cooked risotto for each cake. (Make 6 smaller cakes to serve 6, or 4 larger cakes to serve 4.) Compress the cakes, as you form them, as much as possible, to reduce the possibility of the cakes falling apart during cooking.

5. OVER medium-high heat, heat 2 to 3 tablespoons of the oil in a large, 10-inch skillet, preferably one with a non-stick surface (if the skillet has an uncoated surface, you'll have to add more oil to completely cover the bottom).

When the oil is hot, add the cakes, as many as will fit in the skillet without touching one another, and cook until brown, about 10 minutes on each side.

6. WHILE the risotto cakes are cooking, heat 2 tablespoons of oil in a large skillet over medium-high heat. Add the mushrooms, season with salt and pepper to taste, and cook, stirring, until tender, about 7 minutes. Turn off the heat and set aside.

7. TO SERVE, arrange the risotto cakes on warmed dinner plates and garnish with the mushrooms.

SIMPLE AND SMOOTH

You can make risotto cakes in as many flavors as you make risotto, but you'll get the best results if you use a relatively smooth-textured risotto that's made without big pieces of vegetables, seafood, or meat because chunky texture can cause the risotto cake to break apart during cooking.

Sweet Red Pepper Risotto Cakes with Black Bean Soup

FOR THE SOUP:

2 ounces pancetta, rinsed salt pork, or unsmoked bacon, diced

1 tablespoon olive oil

½ medium-size green bell pepper, cored, seeded, and finely chopped (to yield ½ cup)

1 medium-size onion, peeled and finely chopped

2 large ribs celery, trimmed and finely chopped

2 large cloves garlic, peeled and finely chopped

4 cups cooked black beans, rinsed and drained if canned

1 whole bay leaf

Salt

Pinch red pepper flakes

2 cups chicken broth, preferably homemade (pages 27–28), heated

This recipe was inspired by a luscious dish I tasted at Yuca, one of Miami's updated Cuban restaurants. It makes a wonderful first course, but is hearty enough to serve as a main course.

I always use a pressure cooker to quickly cook the beans and the soup since black beans are just about the hardest of any beans and require the longest cooking time. Use canned beans if you don't want to take the time to soak and cook them.

1. PREPARE the soup: In a large heavy saucepan, heat the pancetta with the olive oil over medium-high heat until the pancetta begins to render its fat, but is not brown, 3 to 5 minutes. Add the green pepper, onion, celery, and garlic and cook, stirring, until the vegetables are softened, about 5 minutes longer. Add the black beans, whole bay leaf, salt and red pepper flakes to taste, and the broth. Cover the pot, turn the heat to high, and bring the liquid to a boil. Reduce the heat to low and cook until the soup has thickened slightly and the flavors combine, about 20 minutes.

2. REMOVE the bayleaf. Transfer the soup to the container of a blender or food processor and blend until smooth. Pour back into the soup pot and set aside. Reheat before serving.

3. MEANWHILE, prepare the risotto cakes: Heat 1 tablespoon of the olive oil in a medium-size, 2- to 3-quart, heavy saucepan with a tight-fitting lid over medium-high heat. Add the onion and the red pepper and cook, stirring, until the onion begins to soften, 2 to 3 minutes. Be careful not to brown it. Stir in the rice to coat the

grains with the oil and onion mixture, and cook about 1 minute longer.

4. ADD 2 cups of the broth and bring the liquid to a boil. Cover the saucepan, turn the heat to low, and cook until the rice is tender but firm, exactly 15 minutes. Turn off the heat.

5. UNCOVER the saucepan and add the remaining ½ cup broth, the cheese, and salt and pepper to taste; stir to combine with the rice. Allow the rice to cool to room temperature. Refrigerate, covered, until completely chilled, at least 3 hours.

6. WHEN the risotto is cold, form into small patty-shaped cakes, using approximately ½ cup of cooked risotto for each cake. (Make 6 smaller cakes to serve 6, or 4 larger cakes to serve 4.) Compress the cakes, as you form them, as much as possible to reduce the possibility of the cakes falling apart during cooking.

7. OVER medium-high heat, heat 2 to 3 tablespoons of oil in a large, 10-inch skillet, preferably one with a nonstick surface (if the skillet has an uncoated surface, you'll have to add more oil to completely cover the bottom). Add the cakes, as many as will fit in the skillet without touching one another, and cook until brown, about 10 minutes on each side.

8. TO SERVE, ladle about ½ cup of the soup into warmed flat soup plates or bowls. Place 1 risotto cake in the center of the plate. Top with a heaping tablespoon of sour cream and garnish with the scallion greens.

FOR THE RISOTTO CAKES:

About ¼ cup olive oil

1 small onion, peeled and finely chopped

½ medium-size red bell pepper, cored, seeded, and finely diced (to yield ½ cup)

1 cup Arborio rice

2 ½ cups chicken broth, preferably homemade (pages 27–28), heated

½ cup freshly grated Italian parmesan cheese

Salt

Freshly ground black pepper

1 cup sour cream

4 scallions, green tops only, chopped

Makes 4 to 6 servings

CHILL OUT

Completely chill the cooked risotto before forming the cakes.

Saffron Risotto Cakes with Roasted Tomatoes

¼ cup olive oil

½ cup finely chopped shallots

1 cup Arborio rice

Pinch of saffron threads, pulverized (see Box, page 99)

2 ½ cups chicken broth, preferably homemade (pages 27–28), heated

½ cup freshly grated Italian parmesan cheese

2 pints ripe cherry tomatoes, cut in half and seeded

Salt

Freshly ground black pepper

Makes 4 to 6 servings

This dish makes a striking visual presentation. The golden yellow color of the risotto cakes are vividly set off by the deep red of the roasted tomatoes.

1. HEAT 1 tablespoon of the oil in a heavy 2- to 3-quart saucepan with a tight-fitting lid over medium-high heat. Add the shallots and cook, stirring, until the shallots begin to soften, 1 to 2 minutes. Be careful not to brown them. Stir in the rice to coat the grains with the oil and shallot mixture, and cook about 1 minute longer.

2. ADD the saffron and 2 cups of the broth and bring the liquid to a boil. Cover the saucepan, turn the heat to low and cook until the rice is tender but firm, exactly 15 minutes. Turn off the heat.

3. UNCOVER the pan and add the remaining ½ cup of the broth, the cheese, and salt and pepper to taste, and stir to combine with the rice. Allow the risotto to cool to room temperature. Refrigerate, covered, until the risotto is completely chilled, at least 3 hours.

4. PREHEAT the oven to 450 degrees.

5. WHILE the risotto is chilling, prepare the tomatoes: Place the tomatoes in a small roasting pan, sprinkle with salt to taste, and drizzle about 1 tablespoon of the olive oil over them; toss well, and place in the preheated oven on the middle shelf. Roast until the watery liquid in the pan cooks away and the tomatoes are tender and soft but not brown, about 20 minutes. Remove from the oven and cover loosely with foil to keep warm.

6. WHEN the risotto is cold, form into small patty-shaped cakes using approximately ½ cup of cooked risotto for each cake. (Make 6 smaller cakes to serve 6, or 4 larger cakes to serve 4.) Compress the cakes, as you form them, as much as possible to reduce the possibility of the cakes falling apart during cooking.

7. OVER medium-high heat, heat 2 to 3 tablespoons of oil in a large, 10-inch skillet, preferably one with a nonstick surface (if the skillet has an uncoated surface, you'll have to add more oil to completely cover the bottom). Add the cakes, as many as will fit in the skillet without touching one another, and cook until brown, about 10 minutes on each side.

8. TO SERVE, arrange the risotto cakes on warmed dinner dishes with some of the roasted tomatoes on the side. Serve immediately.

TIME FOR TURNING

Wait until the risotto cakes are golden brown, 7 to 10 minutes, before you try to turn them. If they are not brown on the bottom, they may break apart during turning.

PORCINI RISOTTO CAKES WITH ARUGULA AND RADICCHIO SALAD

FOR THE RISOTTO CAKES:

1 cup water, boiling

½ ounce dried porcini mushrooms (about ⅓ cup depending on the size of the porcini pieces)

¼ cup olive oil

⅓ cup finely chopped onion

1 cup Arborio rice

2 cups chicken broth, preferably homemade (pages 27–28), heated

½ cup freshly grated Italian parmesan cheese

2 tablespoons finely chopped fresh parsley leaves, rinsed

Salt

Freshly ground black pepper

FOR THE SALAD:

1 bunch arugula, ends trimmed, rinsed in cold water and spun dry

1 small head (about 4 ounces) radicchio, shredded

Salt

2 tablespoons extra-virgin olive oil

1 teaspoon red wine vinegar

Makes 4 to 6 servings

Dried porcini mushrooms impart an intense earthy, mushroomy flavor and aroma to these risotto cakes. The salad offers a tangy contrast to the richness of the cakes. This can be a first or a main course.

1. PREPARE the risotto cakes: Combine the porcini with the boiling water in a heatproof 2-cup glass measuring cup. Allow to stand at least 15 minutes. Drain the porcini and finely chop. Strain the soaking liquid, reserving ½ cup, and add it to the broth. Set aside.

2. HEAT 1 tablespoon of the oil in a medium-size, 2- to 3-quart, heavy saucepan with a tight-fitting lid over medium heat. Add the onion and cook, stirring, until the onion begins to soften, 2 to 3 minutes. Be careful not to brown it. Stir in the rice to coat the grains with the oil and onion mixture, and cook about 1 minute longer. Add the porcini to the rice.

3. ADD 2 cups of the broth mixture to the rice, raise the heat to medium high and bring the liquid to a boil. Cover, reduce the heat to low, and cook until the rice is tender but firm, exactly 15 minutes. Turn off the heat.

4. UNCOVER the saucepan, add the remaining ½ cup broth and the cheese, parsley, and salt and pepper to taste, and stir to combine with the rice. Allow the risotto to cool to room temperature. Refrigerate, covered, until the risotto is completely chilled, at least 3 hours.

5. WHEN the risotto is completely cold, form into small patty-shaped cakes using approximately ½ cup of cooked risotto for each cake. (Make 6 smaller cakes to serve 6,

or 4 larger cakes to serve 4.) Compress the cakes, as you form them, as much as possible to reduce the possibility of the cakes falling apart during cooking.

6. OVER medium-high heat, heat 2 to 3 tablespoons of the oil in a 10-inch skillet, preferably one with a nonstick surface (if the skillet has an uncoated surface, you'll have to add enough oil to completely cover the bottom). Add the cakes, as many as will fit in the skillet without touching one another, and cook until brown, about 10 minutes on each side.

7. COMBINE the arugula and radicchio in a large mixing bowl. Season with salt to taste, add the 2 tablespoons of extra-virgin olive oil and the vinegar and toss well.

8. TO SERVE, arrange the arugula and radicchio salad on plates. Top with the risotto cakes.

NO STICK SKILLET

I like to use a skillet with a nonstick surface for cooking the risotto cakes because you can use as little as 1 to 2 tablespoons of oil—just enough to make a film over the bottom of the pan—to cook the risotto cakes. If you use a skillet with an uncoated surface, you'll have to add more oil to completely cover the bottom of the pan.

Parmigiano-Reggiano Risotto Cakes with Artichoke Ragout

FOR THE RISOTTO CAKES:

¼ cup olive oil

⅓ cup finely chopped onion

1 cup Arborio rice

2 ½ cups chicken broth, preferably homemade (pages 27–28), heated

1 cup freshly grated Italian parmigiano-reggiano cheese

Salt

Freshly ground black pepper

FOR THE ARTICHOKE *RAGÙ*:

2 medium-size artichokes

1 tablespoon olive oil

½ cup finely chopped onion

2 tablespoons finely chopped carrot

1 clove garlic, peeled and pressed or finely chopped

Pinch fennel seed

Juice of ½ lemon

Salt

½ cup water

1 medium-size yellow bell pepper, cut in half, cored and seeded

A simple risotto cake is made exquisitely tasty with this savory artichoke stew served over the cakes to allow the delicious juices to seep down.

1. PREPARE the risotto cakes: Heat 1 tablespoon of the olive oil in a medium-size heavy saucepan with a tight-fitting lid over medium heat. Add the onion and cook, stirring, until the onion begins to soften, 2 to 3 minutes. Be careful not to brown it. Stir in the rice to coat with the oil and onion mixture, and cook about 1 minute longer.

2. ADD 2 cups of the broth, bring to a boil, cover, turn the heat to low and cook until the rice is tender but firm, al dente, exactly 15 minutes. Turn off the heat.

3. UNCOVER the saucepan, add the remaining ½ cup broth, the cheese, and salt and pepper to taste; stir to combine with the rice. Allow the risotto to cool to room temperature. Refrigerate, covered, until the risotto is completely chilled, at least 3 hours.

4. WHILE the risotto is cooling, prepare the artichoke *ragù:* Cut the artichoke stems, leaving about 1 inch from the base. Pull off the tough, dark green leaves, starting with the leaves closest to the stem, until only the yellow-green leaves are visible. Do not use a scissors or knife for this; the leaves will break naturally at the point where the tough part ends and the tender part begins. Using a serrated knife, cut 2 inches off the top of the artichoke, peel the stem, and trim around the base of the artichoke. Cut the artichoke into quarters lengthwise. Cut out the fuzzy choke from each quarter and the spiky sharp leaves just above it. Thinly slice the artichoke bottoms and chop to yield approximately 2 cups.

5. HEAT the oil in a medium-size saucepan over medium heat. Add the onion, carrot, garlic, and fennel seed and cook, stirring, until the onion begins to soften. Add the artichokes, lemon juice, and water, and season with salt to taste. Bring the liquid to a boil, reduce the heat to medium low, and cook, covered, until the artichokes are tender, 15 to 20 minutes.

6. PREHEAT the oven broiler.

7. WHILE the artichokes are cooking, place the yellow pepper halves cut side down on a baking sheet and place in the oven on the top shelf closest to the broiler. Broil until the peppers turn black, about 8 minutes. Remove from the oven, cover the peppers with foil, and allow to stand 10 minutes. Under cold running water, use your fingers to peel the skins from the pepper. Thinly slice the roasted pepper.

8. WHEN the artichokes are tender, add the tomatoes and roasted pepper and cook 5 minutes longer. Season with salt and pepper to taste. Stir in the parsley and set aside. Reheat before serving.

9. WHEN the risotto is cold, form into small patty-shaped cakes using approximately ½ cup of cooked risotto for each cake. (Make 6 smaller cakes to serve 6, or 4 larger cakes to serve 4.) Compress the cakes, as you form them, as much as possible to reduce the possibility of the cakes falling apart during cooking.

10. OVER medium-high heat, heat 2 to 3 tablespoons of the oil in a 10-inch skillet, preferably one with a non-stick surface (if the skillet has an uncoated surface, you'll have to add enough oil to completely cover the bottom). Add the cakes, as many as will fit in the skillet with-out touching one another, and cook until brown, about 10 minutes on each side.

11. To SERVE, arrange 1 cake on each warmed dinner plate and spoon some of the artichoke *ragù* over them. Serve immediately.

2 plum tomatoes, peeled, seeded, and chopped (to yield ¼ cup)

Freshly ground black pepper

2 tablespoons chopped fresh parsley leaves, rinsed

Makes 4 to 6 servings

SPINACH-RISOTTO CAKES WITH MELTED MOZZARELLA CENTERS

¼ cup olive oil

⅓ cup finely chopped onion

1 cup Arborio rice

2 ½ cups chicken broth,
  preferably homemade
  (pages 27–28), heated

⅓ cup freshly grated Italian
  parmesan cheese

2 cups fresh spinach leaves,
  finely chopped; or ¼ cup
  cooked chopped spinach

2 ounces mozzarella cheese,
  preferably fresh, cut into
  2-inch pieces

Salt

Freshly ground black pepper

Makes 4 to 6 servings

These spinach-risotto cakes, like the classic risotto al telephono, have melted mozzarella middles that become stringy when you cut into them and stretch out like telephone wires. These risotto cakes are wonderfully light-tasting. This recipe calls for fresh spinach, but you can also use frozen spinach.

For a different taste try using smoked mozzarella cheese in place of the plain mozzarella. Serve with a tossed green salad as a first course or light entrée.

1. HEAT 1 tablespoon of the olive oil in a medium-size heavy saucepan with a tight-fitting lid over medium-high heat. Add the onion and cook, stirring, until it begins to soften. Be careful not to brown it. Stir in the rice to coat the grains with the oil and onion mixture, and cook about 1 minute longer.

2. ADD 2 cups of the broth and bring the liquid to a boil; reduce the heat to low, cover, and cook until the rice is tender but firm, exactly 15 minutes.

3. UNCOVER the pan, turn off the heat, and add the remaining ½ cup of the broth, the parmesan, spinach, and salt and pepper to taste; stir to combine with the rice. Allow the risotto to cool to room temperature. Refrigerate, covered, until the risotto is completely chilled, at least 3 hours.

4. WHEN the risotto is cold, form into small patty-shaped cakes using approximately ½ cup of cooked risotto for each cake. Insert a piece of the smoked mozzarella into the center of each risotto cake, making sure it is

completely covered with the risotto mixture. (Make 6 smaller cakes to serve 6, or 4 larger cakes to serve 4.) Compress the cakes, as you form them, as much as possible to reduce the possibility of the cakes falling apart during cooking.

5. OVER medium-high heat, heat 2 to 3 tablespoons of the oil in a 10-inch skillet, preferably one with a nonstick surface (if the skillet has an uncoated surface, you'll have to add enough oil to completely cover the bottom). Add the cakes, as many as will fit in the skillet without touching one another, and cook until brown, about 10 minutes on each side. Serve immediately.

CHOOSE CHEESE

Cheese is particularly good for the texture of risotto cakes because it helps to bind and hold the cakes together. In general, you add more parmesan to risotto for cakes than you do in a traditional risotto.

Risotto Cakes with Swiss Chard and Fontina Cheese

¼ cup olive oil

½ cup finely chopped onion

1 cup Arborio rice

2 ½ cups chicken broth, preferably homemade (pages 27–28), heated

1 bunch (1 ½ to 2 pounds) fresh green Swiss chard, ribs cut off and reserved for another use, leaves rinsed in cold water and finely chopped (to yield about ½ cup)

3 ounces Italian fontina cheese, rind removed, diced (to yield about ¾ cup diced)

⅓ cup freshly grated Italian parmesan cheese

Salt

Freshly ground black pepper

Makes 4 to 6 servings

Incredibly luscious, these risotto cakes are irresistible. Serve them with a salad of field greens to make an appealing first course.

1. Heat 1 tablespoon of the olive oil in a medium-size heavy saucepan with a tight-fitting lid over medium-high heat. Add the onion and cook, stirring, until the onion begins to soften, 2 to 3 minutes. Be careful not to brown it. Stir in the rice to coat the grains with oil and onion mixture, and cook about 1 minute longer.

2. Add 2 cups of the broth and bring the liquid to a boil. Cover the saucepan, reduce the heat to low, and cook until the rice is tender but firm, exactly 15 minutes. Turn off the heat.

3. Uncover the pan and add the remaining ½ cup of the broth, the Swiss chard, fontina, parmesan, and salt and pepper to taste; stir to combine with the rice. Allow the risotto to cool to room temperature. Refrigerate, covered, until the risotto is completely chilled, at least 3 hours.

4. When the risotto is cold, form into small patty-shaped cakes using about ½ cup of cooked risotto for each cake. (Make 6 smaller cakes to serve 6, or 4 larger cakes to serve 4.) Compress the cakes, as you form them, as much as possible to reduce the possibility of the cakes falling apart during cooking.

5. Over medium-high heat, heat 2 to 3 tablespoons of oil in a large, 10-inch skillet, preferably one with a nonstick surface (if the skillet has an uncoated surface, you'll have to add more oil to completely cover the bottom). Add the cakes, as many as will fit in the skillet without touching one another, and cook until brown, about 10 minutes on each side. Serve immediately.

TOMATO, BASIL, AND FONTINA RISOTTO CAKES

Serve these creamy, rich, and very flavorful risotto cakes on a bed of greens dressed with a balsamic vinegar dressing.

1. HEAT 1 tablespoon of the olive oil in a medium-size heavy saucepan with a tight-fitting lid over medium-high heat. Add the shallots and cook, stirring, until the shallots begin to soften, 2 to 3 minutes. Be careful not to brown them. Stir in the tomatoes and cook 1 minute. Stir in the rice to coat the grains with the shallot and tomato mixture, and cook about 1 minute longer.

2. ADD 2 cups of the broth and bring the liquid to a boil. Reduce the heat to low, cover the saucepan and cook until the rice is tender but firm, exactly 15 minutes. Turn off the heat.

3. UNCOVER the pan and add the remaining ½ cup of the broth, the fontina, parmesan, basil, salt and pepper to taste; stir to combine with the rice. Allow the risotto to cool to room temperature. Refrigerate, covered, until the risotto is completely chilled, at least 3 hours.

4. WHEN the risotto is cold, form into small patty-shaped cakes using approximately ½ cup of cooked risotto for each cake. (Make 6 smaller cakes to serve 6, or 4 larger cakes to serve 4.) Compress the cakes, as you form them, as much as possible to reduce the possibility of the cakes falling apart during cooking.

5. OVER medium-high heat, heat 2 to 3 tablespoons of the oil in a 10-inch skillet, preferably one with a nonstick surface (if the skillet has an uncoated surface, you'll have to add enough oil to completely cover the bottom). Add the cakes, as many as will fit in the skillet without touching one another, and cook until brown, about 10 minutes on each side. Serve immediately.

¼ cup olive oil

½ cup finely chopped shallots

½ cup chopped canned tomatoes, with their juice

1 cup Arborio rice

2 ½ cups chicken broth, preferably homemade (pages 27–28), heated

4 ounces Italian fontina cheese at room temperature, rind cut off and discarded, cheese cut into ½-inch pieces

½ cup freshly grated Italian parmesan cheese

¼ cup chopped fresh basil leaves

Salt

Freshly ground black pepper

Makes 4 to 6 servings

Sweet Potato and Fontina Risotto Cakes with Mango and Red Onion Salsa

FOR THE RISOTTO CAKES:

¼ cup olive oil

½ cup finely chopped onion

1 clove garlic, peeled and pressed or finely chopped

1 small sweet potato (about 6 ounces), peeled and finely diced

1 cup Arborio rice

2 ½ cups chicken broth, preferably homemade (pages 27–28), heated

4 ounces Italian fontina cheese, rind removed, grated, at room temperature

2 tablespoons freshly grated Italian parmesan cheese

Salt

Freshly ground black pepper

FOR THE SALSA:

½ cup chopped red onion

1 average mango, peeled, seeded, and chopped

2 tablespoons chopped fresh basil leaves

2 tablespoons chopped fresh cilantro

The creamy richness of these risotto cakes is nicely balanced by the zesty salsa. If mangoes are not available, use nectarines or peaches.

1. PREPARE the risotto cakes: Heat 1 tablespoon of the oil in a medium-size heavy saucepan with a tight-fitting lid over medium-high heat. Add the onion, garlic, and potato and cook, stirring, until the onion begins to soften, 2 to 3 minutes. Be careful not to brown it. Stir in the rice to coat the grains with the oil, onion, and potato mixture, and cook about 1 minute longer.

2. ADD 2 cups of the broth and bring the liquid to a boil. Reduce the heat to low, cover, and cook until the rice is tender but firm, exactly 15 minutes. Turn off heat.

3. UNCOVER the pan and add the remaining ½ cup of the broth, the fontina, parmesan, and salt and pepper to taste; stir to combine with the rice. Allow the risotto to cool to room temperature. Refrigerate, covered, until the risotto is completely chilled, at least 3 hours.

4. WHILE the risotto is chilling, prepare the salsa: Combine all the ingredients in a small nonreactive bowl and toss well to combine. Allow to stand at room temperature until ready to serve.

5. WHEN the risotto is cold, form into small patty-shaped cakes using approximately ½ cup of cooked risotto for each cake. (Make 6 smaller cakes to serve 6, or 4 larger cakes to serve 4.) Compress the cakes, as you form them, as much as possible to reduce the possibility of the cakes falling apart during cooking.

6. OVER medium-high heat, heat 2 to 3 tablespoons of the oil in a 10-inch skillet, preferably one with a nonstick surface (if the skillet has an uncoated surface, you'll have to add enough oil to completely cover the bottom). Add the cakes, as many as will fit in the skillet without touching one another, and cook until brown, about 10 minutes on each side.

7. SERVE immediately. Pass the salsa separately.

½ medium-size green bell pepper, cored, seeded, and chopped

Juice of 2 limes

1 teaspoon olive oil

1 teaspoon salt

Makes 4 to 6 servings

WINE NOT?

The basic recipe for risotto cakes calls for 2 ½ cups of cooking liquid. If you want to add wine to the risotto, decrease the amount of cooking liquid accordingly.

Mozzarella Risotto Cakes with Roasted Asparagus

¼ cup olive oil

⅓ cup finely chopped onion

1 cup Arborio rice

2 ½ cups chicken broth,
preferably homemade
(pages 27–28), heated

3 ounces mozzarella cheese, cut
into ½-inch cubes (about
½ cup), at room temperature

⅓ cups freshly grated Italian
parmesan cheese

Salt

Freshly ground black pepper

1 pound thick asparagus spears,
tough bottoms discarded

Makes 4 to 6 servings

This is a simple risotto cake made rich and creamy with mild mozzarella cheese. Use fresh mozzarella if you can find it; it makes a much creamier and even more delicious risotto cake. The roasted asparagus are a tangy complement to the creamy cakes.

1. IN a medium-size heavy saucepan with a tight-fitting lid heat 1 tablespoon of the olive oil over medium-high heat. Add the onion and cook, stirring, until the onion begins to soften, 2 to 3 minutes. Be careful not to brown it. Stir in the rice to coat the grains with the oil and onion mixture, and cook about 1 minute longer.

2. ADD 2 cups of the broth and bring the liquid to a boil. Reduce the heat to low, cover the saucepan and cook until the rice is tender but firm, exactly 15 minutes. Turn off the heat.

3. UNCOVER the pan, add the remaining ½ cup of the broth, the mozzarella, parmesan, and salt and pepper to taste, and stir until the cheeses are melted and combined with the rice. Allow the risotto to cool to room temperature. Refrigerate, covered, until the risotto is completely chilled, at least 3 hours

4. WHEN the risotto is cold, form into small patty-shaped cakes using approximately ½ cup of cooked risotto for each cake. (Make 6 smaller cakes to serve 6, or 4 larger cakes to serve 4.) Compress the cakes, as you form them, as much as possible to reduce the possibility of the cakes falling apart during cooking.

5. PREHEAT the oven to 500 degrees.

6. OVER medium-high heat, heat 2 tablespoons of the oil in a 10-inch skillet, preferably one with a nonstick surface (if the skillet has an uncoated surface, you'll have to add enough oil to completely cover the bottom). Add the cakes, as many as will fit in the skillet without touching one another, and cook until brown, about 10 minutes on each side.

7. WHILE the risotto cakes are cooking, prepare the asparagus: Place the asparagus in a small roasting pan with 1 tablespoon of the oil and stir to coat the spears with the oil. Sprinkle with salt to taste, and place in the oven on the top shelf. Roast 15 minutes. Remove from the oven.

8. TO SERVE, arrange the risotto cakes on warmed dinner plates. Place the roasted asparagus on the side. Serve immediately.

Risotto Cod Cakes with Fennel and Arugula Salad

FOR THE RISOTTO CAKES:

2 cups cold water

1 small onion, peeled and quartered

1 large rib celery

1 teaspoon salt

¼ teaspoon black peppercorns

1 bay leaf

3 sprigs fresh parsley, rinsed

8 ounces fresh cod fillet, or use pollak, flounder, or sole

¼ cup olive oil

½ cup finely chopped onion

1 cup Arborio rice

2 ½ cups chicken broth, preferably homemade (pages 27–28), heated

½ cup chopped fresh basil leaves

2 tablespoons chopped fresh parsley leaves, rinsed

2 tablespoons freshly grated Italian parmesan cheese

Salt

Freshly ground black pepper

Fresh cod lends a delicate taste of fish to these risotto cakes that is wonderfully offset by the refreshing, sharp taste of the fennel and arugula salad.

1. In a medium-size saucepan with a tight-fitting lid, combine the water with the onion, celery, salt, peppercorns, bay leaf, and parsley. Bring the water to a boil over medium-high heat, cover, reduce the heat to low, and cook 10 minutes. Add the cod fillet, cover the saucepan, and cook 10 minutes. Transfer the cod to a plate, cover loosely with foil to help warm, and set aside.

2. Heat 1 tablespoon of the olive oil in a medium-size heavy saucepan with a tight-fitting lid over medium-high heat. Add the onion and cook, stirring, until the onion begins to soften, 2 to 3 minutes. Be careful not to brown it. Stir in the rice to coat the grains with the oil and onion mixture, and cook about 1 minute longer.

3. Add 2 cups of the broth and bring the liquid to a boil. Reduce the heat to low, cover the saucepan and cook until the rice is tender but firm, exactly 15 minutes. Turn off the heat.

4. Uncover the saucepan, add the remaining ½ cup broth and the cod, and beat the mixture with a wooden spoon to combine the fish with the rice, breaking up any large pieces of fish as you stir. When the fish and rice are combined to form a smooth texture, stir in the basil, parsley, parmesan, and salt and pepper to taste; stir to combine with the rice. Allow the risotto to cool to room

temperature. Refrigerate, covered, until the risotto is completely chilled, at least 3 hours.

5. WHEN the risotto is cold, form the risotto into small patty-shaped cakes using approximately ½ cup of cooked risotto for each cake. (Make 6 smaller cakes to serve 6, or 4 larger cakes to serve 4.) Compress the cakes, as you form them, as much as possible to reduce the possibility of the cakes falling apart during cooking.

6. OVER medium-high heat, heat 2 or 3 tablespoons of the oil in a 10-inch skillet, preferably one with a nonstick surface (if the skillet has an uncoated surface, you'll have to add enough oil to completely cover the bottom). Add the cakes, as many as will fit in the skillet without touching one another, and cook until brown, about 10 minutes on each side.

7. WHILE the risotto cakes are cooking, combine the fennel, arugula, and red onion in a large mixing bowl. Season with salt to taste, add the oil and vinegar, and toss well to combine.

8. TO SERVE, pile some of the fennel and arugula salad onto plates and top with 1 or 2 of the risotto cod cakes. Serve immediately.

FOR THE SALAD:

1 small bulb fresh fennel (about 8 ounces) ribs cut off and discarded, bulb cut in half, lengthwise, very thinly sliced crosswise—use a food processor or mandoline if possible

1 bunch arugula, stems trimmed and discarded, rinsed in cold water and spun dry

1 medium-size red onion, peeled and thinly sliced into rounds

Salt

2 tablespoons extra-virgin olive oil

1 teaspoon red wine vinegar

Makes 4 to 6 servings

THREE FISH AND SEAFOOD RISOTTO CAKES

Rice is an ideal partner to the fish and seafood in these risotto cakes. The Italian custom of not combining fish and cheese is sidestepped here; the risotto cakes hold together better with the added parmesan.

RISOTTO CRAB CAKES

1 tablespoon unsalted butter

½ cup finely chopped onion

1 cup Arborio rice

2 ½ cups chicken broth or fish broth, preferably homemade (pages 27–28 and 32–33), heated

8 ounces cooked crab meat, picked over to remove any shells

2 tablespoons freshly grated Italian parmesan cheese

1 tablespoon grated lemon zest

2 tablespoons chopped fresh parsley leaves, rinsed

2 tablespoons chopped scallion greens

Salt

Freshly ground black pepper

2 whole eggs, lightly beaten with 1 tablespoon of water

1 cup plain unseasoned bread crumbs

About 3 tablespoons olive oil

Makes 4 to 6 servings

This recipe is the direct result of my undying affection for crab cakes. As with traditional crab cakes, these risotto crab cakes are flavored with lemon, parsley, and scallion.

Traditional rice croquettes, called suppli *in Italian, are breaded and deep-fried. I found that breading these risotto cakes before they are pan-fried gives them a marvelous crispy crust and helps to hold the cakes together during frying. You can also cook them without any breading.*

1. HEAT the butter in a medium-size heavy saucepan with a tight-fitting lid over medium heat. Add the onion and cook, stirring, until the onion begins to soften, 2 to 3 minutes. Be careful not to brown it. Stir in the rice to coat the grains with the butter and onion mixture, and cook about 1 minute longer.

2. ADD 2 cups of the broth and bring the liquid to a boil. Reduce the heat to low, cover the saucepan and cook until the rice is tender but firm, exactly 15 minutes. Turn off the heat.

3. UNCOVER the saucepan, add the remaining ½ cup broth, the crab, cheese, lemon zest, parsley, scallion greens, and salt and pepper to taste, and stir with a wooden spoon to combine with the rice. Allow the risotto to cool to room temperature. Refrigerate, covered, until the risotto is completely chilled, at least 3 hours.

4. WHEN the risotto is cold, form the risotto into small patty-shaped cakes using approximately ½ cup of cooked risotto for each cake. (Make 6 smaller cakes to serve 6, or 4 larger cakes to serve 4.) Compress the cakes, as you form them, as much as possible to

reduce the possibility of the cakes falling apart during cooking.

5. OVER medium-high heat, heat 2 or 3 tablespoons of the oil in a 10-inch skillet, preferably one with a nonstick surface (if the skillet has an uncoated surface, you'll have to add enough oil to completely cover the bottom). Dip each cake into the beaten egg and then into the bread crumbs, making sure it is completely coated. Place the cakes into the skillet, as many as will fit without touching one another, and cook until brown, about 10 minutes on each side. Serve immediately.

RISOTTO CAKE TIP

If you are preparing risotto especially for risotto cakes, you can skip the stirring and cook the rice, covered, in much the same way you cook ordinary rice. This technique doesn't work for classic risotto because adding all the broth at once and covering the pot means you lose the creamy consistency of risotto, but as you'll see it works just fine for risotto cakes.

ZUCCHINI AND SHRIMP RISOTTO CAKES

¼ cup olive oil

½ cup finely chopped onion

8 ounces zucchini (about
1 medium-size zucchini),
cut into fine julienne strips

1 cup Arborio rice

2 ½ cups chicken broth,
preferably homemade
(pages 27–28), heated

8 ounces small raw shrimp,
peeled (shells reserved),
deveined, and coarsely
chopped

2 tablespoons freshly grated
Italian parmesan cheese

2 tablespoons chopped fresh
parsley leaves, rinsed

Salt

Freshly ground black pepper

Makes 4 to 6 servings

Lightly flavored, these risotto cakes were inspired by a risotto I enjoyed in Italy at the restaurant Cerasole in Cremona. Serve them on a bed of salad greens.

1. HEAT 1 tablespoon of the olive oil in a medium-size heavy saucepan with a tight-fitting lid over medium-high heat. Add the onion and cook, stirring, until the onion begins to soften, 2 to 3 minutes. Be careful not to brown it. Add the zucchini and cook, stirring, 1 minute. Stir in the rice to coat the grains with the oil and onion mixture, and cook about 1 minute longer.

2. ADD 2 cups of the broth and the shrimp, and bring the liquid to a boil. Reduce the heat to low, cover the saucepan and cook until the rice is tender but firm, exactly 15 minutes. Turn off the heat.

3. UNCOVER the pan and add the remaining ½ cup of the broth, the cheese, parsley, and salt and pepper to taste; stir to combine with the rice. Allow the risotto to cool to room temperature. Refrigerate, covered, until the risotto is completely chilled, at least 3 hours.

4. WHEN the risotto is cold, form into small patty-shaped cakes using approximately ½ cup of cooked risotto for each cake. (Make 6 smaller cakes to serve 6, or 4 larger cakes to serve 4.) Compress the cakes, as you form them, as much as possible to reduce the possibility of the cakes falling apart during cooking.

5. OVER medium-high heat, heat 2 or 3 tablespoons of the oil in a 10-inch skillet, preferably one with a nonstick surface (if the skillet has an uncoated surface, you'll have to add more oil to completely cover the bottom). Add the cakes, as many as will fit in the skillet without touching one another, and cook until brown, about 10 minutes on each side. Serve with a green salad.

chapter **NINE**

Riceless
"risotto"

$\mathcal{T}$echnically speaking, none of these recipes qualifies as *real* risotto since there isn't a single grain of rice in any of them, and a true risotto is, as the name implies, a rice dish. But cooks today have found that the technique for preparing risotto can be applied to other grains as well as to vegetables; cooking them in butter or oil with onion or shallot and adding broth gradually to slowly cook them—the way it's done for risotto—produces a delicious dish that is risottolike.

Of the many chefs I talked to who prepare riceless "risotti," or *faux* risotto as it is also called, Michel Richard, the chef and co-owner of the restaurant Citrus in Los Angeles, is one of the most adventurous. He makes "risotti" with just about every vegetable, including celery, carrot, potato, asparagus, and even apple for dessert (see page 199). He says his "risotti" are fun and provide a different way to serve vegetables.

But even in Italy, where there is not much invention when it comes to cooking risotto, there are riceless "risotti." In the regions where barley is grown, barley is prepared as a "risotto," and that distinctive Tuscan specialty, *farro*, a variety of whole wheat, is also prepared as a "risotto." These preparations are not new there.

Most of these recipes cook up relatively quickly, in about 15 minutes, and require considerably less broth than traditional risotto. Wherever chicken broth has been called for in the recipe, you can substitute a vegetarian broth (see pages 30–31).

Most riceless "risotti" are best when served as an accompaniment to meat or fish. Only the grains—barley, *farro*, pasta, and wild rice—can be served like a real risotto, as a first course or as a light entrée.

Michel Richard's Potato "Risotto" with Pancetta

This dish should be served as an accompaniment to roasted or grilled meat as you would serve any other potatoes. The texture is surprisingly like risotto, but the flavor is all spud. Richard uses only Yukon Gold potatoes; they hold up particularly well to this cooking technique and keep their grainlike texture. If pancetta is not available, use a good quality bacon.

2 ounces pancetta, cut into small dice

2 tablespoons unsalted butter

¼ cup finely chopped shallot

2 pounds boiling potatoes, preferably Yukon Gold, peeled and cut into ⅛-inch dice

2 cups chicken broth, preferably homemade (pages 27–28), heated

½ cup freshly grated Italian parmesan cheese

Salt

Freshly ground black pepper

Makes 6 servings

1. PLACE the pancetta in a 2- to 3-quart heavy saucepan over medium-high heat. Cook the pancetta, stirring, until all the pieces are well-browned but not burned, 5 to 7 minutes. Remove the pancetta with a slotted spoon and set aside.

2. POUR off all but 1 tablespoon of the fat. Add the butter to the pan. When the butter is bubbling, add the shallots and cook over medium heat until softened, 2 to 3 minutes. Be careful not to brown them. Add the potatoes and stir to combine.

3. ADD the broth, a few tablespoons at a time, stirring well after each addition until it is mostly absorbed by the potatoes. Continue to add the broth a few tablespoons at a time, while stirring, until the potatoes are tender and the texture is creamy smooth, about 15 minutes. Stir in the cheese and cooked pancetta and season with salt and pepper to taste. Serve immediately.

Tra Vigne's Potato and Squash "Risotto"

2 tablespoons unsalted butter

1 tablespoon olive oil

½ cup finely chopped onion

1 large clove garlic, peeled and pressed or finely chopped

1 pound boiling potatoes, preferably Yukon Gold, peeled and cut into very small dice (to yield 2 cups)

4 ounces peeled butternut squash, cut into very small dice (to yield 1 cup)

6 sprigs fresh thyme, chopped; or ½ teaspoon dried thyme

Pinch fennel seeds

2 cups chicken broth, preferably homemade (pages 27–28), heated

1 cup packed fresh spinach leaves, rinsed, stemmed, dried, and roughly chopped

½ cup freshly grated Italian parmesan cheese

Salt

Freshly ground black pepper

Makes 6 servings

This is one of the best riceless risotti there is. It comes from California's Napa Valley restaurant Tra Vigne, where chef/owner Michael Chiarello serves this hearty dish as an accompaniment to roasted baby chicken, poussin.

1. COMBINE 1 tablespoon of the butter with the oil in a heavy 4-quart pot, preferably enameled cast iron, over medium-high heat. Add the onion and garlic and cook, stirring, until the onion begins to soften, 2 to 3 minutes. Be careful not to brown it. Add the potatoes and squash and stir to coat the potato and squash with the onion and butter mixture, and cook about 1 minute longer.

2. ADD the thyme and fennel seeds, and begin to add the broth, a few tablespoons at a time, stirring well after each addition. Continue to add the broth in small amounts and cook, stirring, until the potatoes and squash are tender and creamy, 15 to 20 minutes.

3. ADD the spinach, the remaining tablespoon of butter, and the cheese and continue stirring until the butter is melted and the cheese has been incorporated into the potato "risotto." Season with salt and pepper to taste. Serve immediately.

BARLEY AND PORCINI MUSHROOM "RISOTTO"

Of all the grains, barley that's cooked in the manner of a risotto is the most like a real risotto both in texture and consistency. Because barley is a harder grain than rice, it requires some precooking.

1. COMBINE the porcini with the boiling water in a heat-proof 2-cup glass measuring cup. Allow to stand at least 15 minutes. Drain the porcini, reserving the soaking liquid, and finely chop. Strain the soaking liquid, combine ½ cup with the broth in a small saucepan, and heat over medium-low heat.

2. WHILE the porcini are soaking, place the barley, with salt to taste, in a medium-size saucepan with enough water to amply cover it, and bring the liquid to a boil over medium-high heat. Reduce the heat to low and cook until the barley is almost tender, about 20 minutes. Drain and set aside.

3. HEAT 1 tablespoon of the butter with the olive oil in a heavy 4-quart pot over medium-high heat. Add the onion, carrot, and celery and cook, stirring, until the vegetables begin to soften, 2 to 3 minutes. Be careful not to brown them. Add the drained barley and stir to combine with the vegetables.

4. ADD the broth and porcini liquid mixture, ½ cup at a time, stirring well after each addition until the broth has been absorbed by the barley.

5. WHEN the barley is tender and the liquid is thickened and creamy, in about 15 minutes, turn off the heat. Add the remaining tablespoon of butter, the parsley, cheese, and salt and pepper to taste and stir to combine with the barley. Serve immediately.

1 ounce dried porcini mushrooms (about ⅔ cup depending on the size of the porcini pieces)

1 cup water, boiling

4 cups chicken broth, preferably homemade (pages 27–28), heated

1 cup pearl barley

Salt

2 tablespoons unsalted butter

2 tablespoons olive oil

⅓ cup finely chopped onion

1 small carrot, peeled and finely chopped

1 rib celery, trimmed and finely chopped

¼ cup chopped fresh parsley leaves, rinsed

⅓ cup freshly grated Italian parmesan cheese

Freshly ground pepper to taste

Makes 6 servings

WILD RICE "RISOTTO"

One 6-ounce package,
  unseasoned, wild rice

4 cups water

Salt

1 small potato (4 ounces),
  preferably russet, peeled and
  cut into quarters

¼ cup milk

2 tablespoons olive oil

½ cup finely chopped onion

¼ cup finely chopped carrot

2 cloves garlic, peeled and
  pressed or finely chopped

2 cups chicken broth,
  preferably homemade
  (pages 27–28), heated

⅓ cup freshly grated Italian
  parmesan cheese

⅓ cup chopped fresh parsley
  leaves, rinsed

Freshly ground black pepper

Makes 4 servings

Wild rice is technically not rice at all but a grass, zizania aquatica, that grows in the northern regions of the American Midwest. Most wild rice found in supermarkets today is cultivated in Minnesota and harvested by hand. There are different grades of wild rice: the best is the fancy long grain; to be avoided are the broken leftovers that are also sold. Be careful not to buy wild rice mixes or wild rice that is packaged with ordinary rice; they won't give you the results you want in this recipe.

Because wild rice doesn't have any natural starchiness, I found that the addition of a little bit of mashed potato gives this riceless "risotto" just the right creamy, smooth texture you'd expect in a real risotto.

1. POUR the wild rice into a small saucepan with the water and 1 teaspoon salt. Place over high heat and bring the water to a boil. Reduce the heat to low and simmer uncovered until the wild rice is tender and the grains have mostly opened, about 50 minutes. Drain and set aside.

2. MEANWHILE, place the potato in a separate small saucepan with enough water to cover and set over high heat. Bring the water to a boil, reduce the heat to low, and cook until the potato is completely tender when pierced with a sharp knife, about 20 minutes. Drain; peel the potato pieces and place them in a small mixing bowl. Use a fork to mash the potato; add the milk gradually, beating with the fork, until the potato is smooth. Set aside.

3. HEAT the oil in a heavy 4-quart pot over medium-high heat. Add the onion, carrot, and garlic and cook until

the vegetables begin to soften, 2 to 3 minutes. Be careful not to brown them. Add the drained wild rice and stir to combine the rice and vegetables, and cook about 1 minute longer.

4. ADD the broth, ½ cup at a time, stirring well after each addition until the broth has mostly been absorbed by the rice.

5. WHEN all the broth has been added and the rice is completely tender, in about 15 minutes, turn off the heat. Stir in ¼ cup of the mashed potato, the cheese, and parsley and stir well to combine with rice. Season with salt and pepper to taste. Serve immediately.

Farro "Risotto" with Spring Vegetables and Roasted Asparagus

1 ¼ pounds thin asparagus
spears, bottoms trimmed;
1 pound left whole, spears
peeled; 4 ounces (about
6 spears) finely chopped

3 tablespoons olive oil

Salt

½ cup finely chopped onion

1 large clove garlic, peeled and
pressed or finely chopped

¼ cup finely chopped carrot

1 cup whole farro

½ cup cracked farro

4 cups chicken broth,
preferably homemade
(pages 27–28), heated

1 small zucchini (about 8
ounces), cut into small dice

1 cup fresh baby fava beans,
shelled and peeled (optional,
if available)

½ cup freshly grated Italian
parmesan cheese

Freshly ground black pepper

Makes 6 servings

Farro, a hard and deliciously nutty-flavored variety of whole wheat, was a staple of ancient Roman cuisine, and is one of the oldest known varieties of wheat still being cultivated today. Farro's popularity is concentrated primarily in Tuscany in Italy and specifically in the area around Lucca where zuppa al farro and farro risotto are traditionally prepared.

The inspiration for this recipe comes from the California restaurant Tra Vigne, where they call their farro risotto, "Over the Hill Risotto." Farro can be found in Italian specialty food stores. This recipe calls for both whole and cracked farro.

1. PREHEAT the oven to 500 degrees.

2. PREPARE the asparagus: Set the chopped asparagus aside. Place the peeled whole spears in a small roasting pan. Coat with 1 tablespoon of the olive oil, sprinkle with salt to taste, and roast in the oven for 15 minutes. Remove from the oven, cover loosely with foil to keep warm, and set aside.

3. HEAT the remaining 2 tablespoons of the oil in a 4-quart heavy pot over medium-high heat. Add the onion, garlic, and carrot and cook, stirring, until the onion begins to soften, 2 to 3 minutes. Be careful not to brown it. Add the whole and cracked farro and stir to coat the grains with the oil and onion mixture, and cook about 1 minute longer.

4. ADD the broth, ½ cup at a time, stirring well after each addition until the broth has mostly been absorbed by the farro.

5. WHEN the farro is tender but firm, in about 30 minutes, add the chopped asparagus, zucchini, and baby fava beans and continue cooking 5 minutes longer. Stir in the cheese and salt and pepper to taste.

6. TO SERVE, arrange the roasted asparagus on warmed dinner plates. Spoon the farro risotto over the asparagus. Serve immediately.

Pastina "Risotto" with Pancetta, Shiitake Mushrooms, and Frisée

3 tablespoons brown lentils or French *lentilles vertes du Puy* or the Italian *lenticche di Castelluccio*

1 tablespoon unsalted butter

4 ounces shiitake mushrooms, stemmed, caps thinly sliced

Salt

Freshly ground black pepper

4 ounces pancetta, coarsely chopped

1 tablespoon olive oil

½ cup finely chopped onion

¼ cup finely chopped carrot

1 large clove garlic, peeled and pressed or finely chopped

1 cup large pastina pasta, preferably *acini di pepe*

4 cups chicken broth, preferably homemade (pages 27–28), heated

¼ cup chopped fresh parsley leaves, rinsed

⅓ cup freshly grated Italian parmesan cheese

Makes 6 servings

Small pasta shapes have enough starch to thicken the broth and make a very risottolike dish. Even though pasta usually cooks in 10 minutes, when cooking with the risotto technique, the cooking time is longer.

1. PLACE the lentils in a small saucepan, with enough water to cover, over medium-high heat. Bring the water to a boil, reduce the heat to low, and cook until the lentils are tender, 25 to 30 minutes. Drain and set aside.

2. IN a small skillet heat the butter over medium heat. Add the mushrooms, season with salt and pepper to taste, and cook, stirring, until tender, about 7 minutes. Turn off the heat and set aside.

3. PUT the pancetta in a heavy 4-quart pot over medium-high heat. Cook the pancetta until the pieces are well browned and most of the fat has been rendered, about 5 minutes. Use a slotted spoon to remove the pieces of pancetta.

4. POUR off all but 1 tablespoon of the fat. Add the oil; stir in the onion, carrot, and garlic and cook, stirring, until the onion begins to soften, 2 to 3 minutes. Be careful not to brown it. Stir in the pastina to coat with the fat and onion mixture, and cook about 1 minute longer.

5. ADD the broth, ½ cup at a time, stirring well after each addition until most of the broth has been absorbed by the pasta.

6. WHEN the pasta is tender but firm, in about 20 minutes, turn off the heat. Add the lentils, mushrooms, pancetta, parsley, cheese, and enough broth to give the "risotto" a smooth texture, and stir to combine. Season with salt and pepper to taste. Serve immediately.

Orzo Pasta "Risotto" with Parsley and Pecorino Romano Cheese

1. HEAT the olive oil in a heavy saucepan, preferably one with a nonstick surface, over medium-high heat. Add the onion; cook, stirring, until the onion begins to soften, 2 to 3 minutes. Be careful not to brown it. Stir in the orzo to coat with the onion and oil mixture, and cook about 1 minute longer.

2. ADD the broth, ½ cup at a time, stirring well after each addition.

3. WHEN the orzo is tender and most of the liquid has been absorbed by the pasta, in about 20 minutes, turn off the heat. Add the parsley and cheese, and continue stirring until the cheese and parsley are well combined with the pasta, 1 to 2 minutes longer. Season to taste with salt and pepper. Serve immediately.

1 tablespoon olive oil

¼ cup finely chopped onion

1 cup orzo pasta

4 cups chicken broth, preferably homemade (pages 27–28), heated

¼ cup finely chopped fresh parsley leaves

⅓ cup freshly grated pecorino romano cheese

Salt

Freshly ground pepper

Makes 4 servings

Mixed Vegetable "Risotto" with Basil

1 tablespoon olive oil

2 tablespoons unsalted butter

½ cup finely chopped onion

1 large clove garlic, peeled and pressed or finely chopped

1 small carrot (about 4 ounces), ends trimmed, finely diced

1 large rib of celery, ends trimmed, finely diced

1 small zucchini (about 8 ounces), ends trimmed, finely diced

1 small yellow squash (about 8 ounces), ends trimmed, finely diced

1 medium-size russet potato (about 8 ounces), peeled and finely diced

1 medium-size sweet potato (about 8 ounces), peeled and finely diced

2 cups chicken broth, preferably homemade (pages 27–28), heated

¼ cup chopped fresh basil leaves

⅓ cup freshly grated Italian parmesan cheese

Salt

Freshly ground black pepper

Makes 4 servings

A colorful mix of different vegetables makes this "risotto" a superb side dish to accompany any main course, whether meat, fish, or fowl. Be sure to dice or chop the vegetables very finely, as it gives the dish a more conventional risotto texture.

1. HEAT the oil and 1 tablespoon of the butter in a heavy 4-quart pot over medium-high heat. Add the onion, garlic, carrot, and celery and cook, stirring, until the vegetables begin to soften, 2 to 3 minutes. Be careful not to brown them. Stir in the zucchini, yellow squash, and potatoes to coat with the fat and onion mixture, and cook about 1 minute.

2. ADD the broth, ¼ cup at a time, stirring well after each addition until it is mostly absorbed by the vegetable mixture.

3. WHEN the mixture is thick and the vegetables are tender, in 10 to 15 minutes, turn off the heat. Stir in the basil, cheese, and remaining tablespoon of butter. Season with salt and pepper to taste. Serve immediately.

Sweet Corn "Risotto"

The idea for this recipe came from Joachim Splichal, the chef and owner of the Los Angeles restaurant Patina. An updated creamed corn, this "risotto" is a great accompaniment to roast chicken or loin of pork.

1. USING a small, sharp paring knife, preferably one with a serrated edge, cut the kernels from the ears. You should have 2 ½ to 3 cups of kernels. Set aside.

2. IN a medium-size saucepan, heat the butter over medium heat. Add the shallots and cook until they begin to soften, 2 to 3 minutes. Be careful not to brown them. Stir in the corn kernels to coat them with the butter and shallot mixture, and cook about 1 minute longer.

3. ADD the half-and-half, ¼ cup at a time, stirring well after each addition until the liquid has reduced by about half.

4. WHEN the corn is tender and the liquid has thickened, in about 10 minutes, turn off the heat. Stir in the parsley; season with salt and pepper to taste. Serve immediately.

4 medium-size ears sweet summer corn, shucked and desilked

1 tablespoon unsalted butter

¼ cup finely chopped shallots

1 cup half-and-half, heated

1 tablespoon chopped fresh parsley, rinsed

Salt

Freshly ground black pepper

Makes 4 servings

chapter TEN

Dessert
Risotti

$\mathscr{S}$weet rice desserts and confections have a place in many culinary traditions. In northern Italy, you find rice custard and tarts—but not sweet risotti, per se—that are prepared with the rice that grows in the Po River valley. There is nothing as comforting, soothing, and just plain delicious as rice desserts or sweet risotti.

SWEET BAKED RISOTTO PUDDING WITH ORANGE, VANILLA, AND RAISINS

This rich risotto is reminiscent of a traditional rice pudding, but the al dente grains of rice make it distinctive. You can lighten this recipe by using low-fat milk in place of the whole milk, and milk instead of the cream.

1. PREHEAT the oven to 425 degrees.

2. HEAT the butter in a heavy 4-quart flameproof casserole with a tight-fitting lid over medium heat. When the butter is bubbling, add the orange zest and the rice, stir to coat the grains of rice with the butter, and cook about 1 minute.

3. ADD the vanilla, the raisins, and the milk; raise the heat to medium-high and bring the milk to a simmer on top of the stove. Cover the casserole and place on the middle shelf in the oven. Bake for 30 minutes.

4. REMOVE the casserole from the oven and allow the rice to cool to room temperature. Stir in ½ cup of the cream and refrigerate for several hours or overnight. Before serving, stir in the remaining ½ cup of cream.

2 tablespoons unsalted butter

1 teaspoon grated orange zest

1 cup Arborio rice

1 teaspoon vanilla extract

½ cup dark raisins

3 cups whole milk, heated

1 cup heavy cream

Makes 6 servings

LULU'S SWEET RISOTTO TART WITH LEMON AND VANILLA

FOR THE CRUST:

1 cup unbleached white flour, plus additional for rolling out the dough

2 teaspoons granulated sugar

8 tablespoons (1 stick) frozen or cold unsalted butter, cut into 8 pieces

⅓ cup ice water

FOR THE RISOTTO FILLING:

2 tablespoons unsalted butter

1 teaspoon grated lemon zest

1 cup Arborio rice

1 teaspoon vanilla extract

⅓ cup granulated sugar

4 cups half-and-half, heated

Makes 8 servings

Reed Herron, the San Francisco chef and restaurateur, serves this risotto tart at his bistro, Lulu Bis. The rice is mostly cooked on top of the stove before it is baked in a flaky pastry crust in the oven.

1. PREPARE the crust: Combine the flour and sugar in the bowl of a food processor fitted with the metal blade. Process 10 seconds to combine. Add the butter and process until the butter is reduced to mostly pea-size pieces, about 30 seconds. With the machine running, gradually add the water in a stream. Process until the dough forms a ball on the blade. Remove the dough from the processor, wrap in plastic or wax paper, and press it into a disk shape. Refrigerate for at least 30 minutes.

2. ROLL the dough out on a well-floured surface with a floured rolling pin. Press into a 9-inch tart pan with a removeable bottom or a ceramic quiche dish with fluted sides. Refrigerate or freeze until ready to fill.

3. PREHEAT the oven to 425 degrees.

4. PREPARE the risotto filling: Heat the butter in a small heavy saucepan over medium heat. Add the lemon zest and cook about 1 minute. Stir in the rice to coat the grains with the butter and lemon zest mixture, and cook about 1 minute longer.

5. ADD the vanilla, sugar, and 2 cups of the half-and-half. Turn the heat to low, cook, stirring frequently, until most of the cream has been absorbed by the rice, about 10 minutes. Add 1 more cup of the cream and continue

cooking 10 minutes longer. Add the remaining cup of cream and cook 10 minutes longer.

6. Pour the risotto into the prepared crust and place on the middle rack in the oven. Bake 30 minutes. Remove the tart from the oven and allow to cool 15 minutes before serving.

SWEET RISOTTO WITH FRESH FRUIT COMPOTE

FOR THE FRUIT:

2 ½ pounds fresh peaches
(or other seasonal fruit)

Juice of ½ lemon

¼ cup granulated sugar

2 tablespoons water

⅓ cup Vin Santo or other sweet
wine

FOR THE RISOTTO:

2 ½ cups whole milk

¼ cup granulated sugar

4 tablespoons unsalted butter

1 cup Arborio rice

⅓ cup golden raisins, soaked in
warm water

⅓ cup slivered or chopped
almonds

Makes 4 servings

*This recipe is from California chef Rick O'Connell, who invented
it as a breakfast entrée. It also makes a wonderful dessert.*

1. PREPARE the fruit: Place the peaches in boiling water for
   1 minute; drain and peel.

2. CUT the peeled peaches in half and then into ½-inch
   wedges. Place in a small nonreactive saucepan with the
   lemon juice, sugar, and water. Cook until the fruit is tender and the cooking liquid is syrupy, about 10 to 15
   minutes. Add the wine and cook 1 minute longer. Set
   aside.

3. PREPARE the risotto: Place the sugar and milk in a medium-
   size saucepan over medium heat and heat until bubbles
   begin to appear around the edge. Turn off the heat.

4. IN a heavy 2-quart saucepan, heat 2 tablespoons of
   the butter over medium-high heat until melted and
   bubbling. Stir in the rice to coat the grains with the
   butter, and cook about 1 minute longer.

5. GRADUALLY add the milk, ½ cup at a time, stirring well
   after each addition. Wait until each addition is almost
   completely absorbed before adding the next ½ cup.

6. WHEN the rice is tender but firm, in about 25 minutes,
   turn off the heat. Stir in the raisins, nuts, remaining butter, and cream. Serve immediately topped with the fruit
   compote.

LOW-FAT FALL FRUIT RISOTTO

In this low-fat dessert risotto, dried fruit and apples are cooked with rice and cider to become a barely sweet confection that makes the perfect ending to a hearty fall meal. For a richer dessert, serve this risotto with vanilla ice cream or frozen yogurt.

1. COMBINE the dried fruit in a large glass measuring cup with 1 cup of the cider and allow to stand 15 minutes.

2. IN a heavy 2-quart saucepan, heat the butter over medium-high heat until melted and bubbling. Stir in the rice to coat the grains with the butter, about 1 minute.

3. ADD the orange and lemon zests and the Marsala and cook, stirring, until the Marsala is mostly absorbed by the rice. Add the apple, dried fruit, and the cider in which it was soaking and stir until the cider has mostly been absorbed by the rice. Continue adding the cider, ¼ cup at a time, stirring well after each addition. Wait until each addition is almost completely absorbed before adding the next ¼ cup.

4. WHEN the rice is tender but firm, in about 20 minutes, stir in the sugar and vanilla extract. Allow the risotto to cool to room temperature before serving.

¼ cup (2 ounces) dried cranberries or cherries, chopped

¼ cup (2 ounces) dried currants

½ cup (2 ounces) dried apricots, chopped

2 ½ cups apple cider, heated

1 tablespoon unsalted butter or canola, corn, or other vegetable oil

1 cup Arborio rice

1 ½ teaspoons grated orange zest

1 teaspoon grated lemon zest

½ cup dry Marsala wine

1 medium-size apple, preferably Granny Smith, peeled, cored, and diced (to yield 1 ½ cups)

2 tablespoons granulated sugar

½ teaspoon vanilla extract

Makes 6 servings

SWEET RISOTTO CAKES WITH PISTACHIO CRUST

2 tablespoons unsalted butter

1 teaspoon grated orange zest

1 cup Arborio rice

½ cup granulated sugar

1 teaspoon vanilla extract

3 ½ cups whole milk, heated

½ cup mascarpone cheese

1 whole large egg, beaten

½ cup unbleached white flour

1 cup finely chopped unsalted shelled pistachio nuts

2 tablespoons canola, corn, or other vegetable oil

1 pint vanilla ice cream

Makes 6 servings

You can use leftover Sweet Baked Risotto Pudding with Orange, Vanilla, and Raisins (page 193) to prepare these sweet cakes, but this recipe with creamy mascarpone makes the cakes extraordinary.

1. HEAT the butter in a medium-size heavy saucepan over medium heat. When the butter is melted and bubbly, add the orange zest and cook 1 minute. Stir in the rice and the sugar to coat the grains with the butter, about 1 minute longer.

2. ADD the vanilla and 3 cups of the milk and bring the liquid to a boil. Turn the heat to low and cook, stirring occasionally to prevent sticking and lumping, for 20 minutes. Add the remaining ½ cup of milk and cook, stirring, 10 minutes.

3. TAKE the pan from the heat and allow the rice mixture to cool to room temperature. Stir in the mascarpone and chill for at least 3 hours or overnight.

4. PREHEAT the oven to 400 degrees.

5. WHEN the risotto is chilled, form the risotto into patty-shaped cakes using about ½ cup for each cake. Put the egg, flour, and nuts into 3 separate bowls. Dip the cakes first into the beaten egg to thoroughly coat them, then into the flour, dusting off any excess, and finally into the pistachio nuts, pressing the nuts to the surface of the cakes to help them adhere.

6. HEAT the oil in a medium-size ovenproof skillet over medium heat. Place the risotto cakes in the pan and cook 1 minute. Turn the cakes over and place the skillet immediately into the oven. Bake for 5 minutes. Remove and serve immediately with vanilla ice cream.

APPLE "RISOTTO"

This recipe was inspired by an apple "risotto" I was served at the Los Angeles restaurant, Citrus, by chef Michel Richard. The apples are finely diced and cooked until almost a pudding. Serve this dessert "risotto" warm with vanilla ice cream.

1. HEAT the butter in a medium-size heavy saucepan over medium heat. When the butter is melted and bubbling, add the apples, sugar, and lemon juice and cook, stirring with a wooden spoon, until the natural liquid from the apples has mostly cooked away, 10 to 12 minutes.

2. BEGIN to add the cider a few tablespoons at a time, stirring well after each addition. Continue to add the cider until it has all been added and the diced apples are tender and the risotto is thick, about 10 minutes. Allow to cool slightly. Serve warm with vanilla ice cream.

2 tablespoons unsalted butter

8 cups finely diced peeled, seeded, and cored Granny Smith apples (about 8 apples)

½ cup granulated sugar

Juice of ½ lemon

1 cup apple cider, heated

Makes 6 servings

INDEX